When FOOTBALL Was FOOTBALL

DERBY COUNTY

First published in 2013

A catalogue record for this book is available from the British Library

ISBN: 978-0-85733-193-9

Published by Haynes Publishing, Sparkford, Yeovil,
Somerset BA22 7JJ, UK
Tel: 01963 442030 Fax: 01963 440001
Int. tel: +44 1963 442030 Int. fax: +44 1963 440001
E-mail: sales@haynes.co.uk
Website: www.haynes.co.uk

Haynes North America Inc., 861 Lawrence Drive,
Newbury Park, California 91320, USA

Images © Mirrorpix

Creative Director: Kevin Gardner
Designed for Haynes by BrainWave

Printed and bound in the US

When FOOTBALL *Was* FOOTBALL

DERBY COUNTY

A Nostalgic Look at a Century of the Club

Tom Hopkinson

Contents

Foreword

When I closed the door behind Brian Clough and Peter Taylor in the early hours of a Saturday morning in 1967, I knew my life was going to change forever.

Brian and Peter had come to persuade me to sign for Derby County Football Club, and what stands out from the conversation we had that night is the fact they promised it would be a journey. They promised it would change my life – and it did.

The things they talked about and forecast actually happened. It is great to be in Derby County's record books: I am so proud to have been part of two championship-winning sides and I never thought in a million years I would play for England.

They said I would do that within 12 months. In reality, it was about 15 or 16 before I played for the Under-23s, but it was still extraordinary what happened from that moment.

Not that I had much choice. Brian and Peter could be quite persuasive and, had I said "No", the pair of them would probably still be in my house now.

They convinced me to move from Liverpool to Derby and, 45 years on, I'm still here. My wife's from Derby, my daughter's from Derby and my two grandchildren were born here, so I've no reason to leave.

I'm stuck here and I love the place, and my association with Derby County and its

supporters is one I hope I will have for the rest of my life.

Along the way there have been some not very nice times as well, but that's part and parcel of football and life, and you have to accept that.

And there have been so many more fabulous times: the magical European nights in the Seventies – Benfica, Juventus and Real Madrid – were special, and the games I played for England were some of the proudest moments of my life. I was representing Derby County every time I did that.

During my time as a player at Derby and through almost all of the club's rich history, the *Mirror* and its sister papers have been there to report on the great games and great players, and the heartbreaking moments as well. The evocative pictures – taken from the *Mirror* archive – which feature in this book have rekindled so many wonderful memories of the matches I played in, the people I played with and against, or worked with at the club and knew, and I hope they will rekindle your memories as well.

This is a celebration of a golden age for football and a fine portrait of a wonderful club.

Roy McFarland

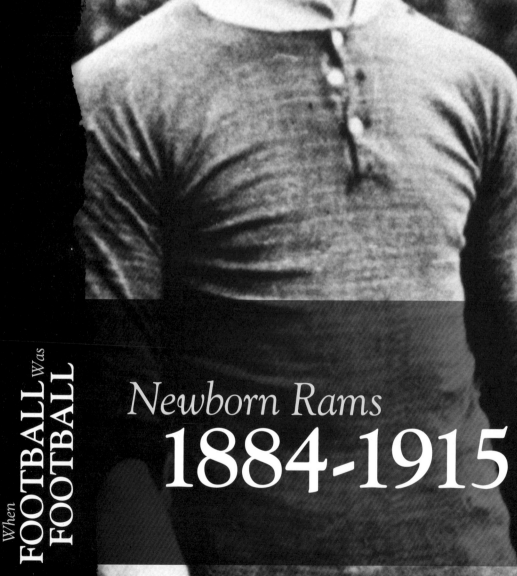

Newborn Rams
1884-1915

It is a thought inconceivable to many in Derbyshire today, but for 1,884 years there was no football club upon which the county folk could pin their hopes and dreams. A gentleman by the name of William Morley changed all that, though, when – spurred on by his namesake son – he struck upon the idea of forming a football offshoot of Derbyshire County Cricket Club, which would not only give the locals a team to support in the winter months but generate some much-needed revenue for those who wielded the willow during the good old British summertime.

And so, out of Morley's vision, the Rams were born. The club took part in an extensive programme of friendly fixtures, playing their home games at the Racecourse Ground they shared with their cricketing cousins, before accepting an invitation, in 1888, to become one of the 12 founder members of the Football League. In 1895, by which time Derby had done away with their previous colours of chocolate, amber and pale blue in favour of white and black, the club made the Baseball Ground their permanent home and, during their 102-year stay at the stadium, they established themselves as one of the biggest and best-loved football clubs in England.

Steve Bloomer (right) was one of the most potent forwards in the Football League during its formative years. The Derby striker – pictured here in the early 1900s with Billy Meredith, then of Manchester United – was often referred to as the best goalscorer of his generation.

> *Because goals count for more than anything, when considering the respective merits of all the international inside-forwards, I would always give the palm to my old friend Steve.*
>
> Billy Meredith

1884 Derby County Football Club is formed as an offshoot of Derbyshire County Cricket Club, which was itself formed in 1871. **1888** The Football League is formed, with Derby County one of its 12 founding members. Preston North End, Bolton, West Bromwich Albion, Everton, Accrington Stanley, Stoke, Notts County, Wolves, Blackburn, Aston Villa and Burnley complete the list. Derby beat Bolton 6-3 in their first game and finish the season 10ᵗʰ. **1892** Derby use the Baseball Ground for the first time when a race meeting at the club's original home, the Racecourse Ground, clashes with a home game against Sunderland on 19ᵗʰ March. Derby lose 1-0. The same year, Steve Bloomer makes his debut at the age of 18. **1895** The Rams finish second, four points behind champions Villa, and reach the semi-finals of the FA Cup. **1898** Derby reach the FA Cup final, held at Crystal Palace, for the first time, but lose 3-1 to local rivals Nottingham Forest. An unwanted double is achieved when the Rams lose their second successive FA Cup final, this time 4-1 to Sheffield United.

By the time the *Mirror* launched in November 1903, the Rams had established themselves as one of the biggest clubs in England. There was still no silverware, but the club would regularly reach the later stages of the FA Cup, and three times were losing finalists at Crystal Palace, where the showpiece was then played. In the Football League, Derby finished third on three occasions and second, to Aston Villa, in 1896. More often, though, they would finish in mid-table, with inconsistent performances largely to blame.

How the Mirror covered Derby in the early years

RIGHT: The first surviving mention of Derby County in the pages of the *Daily Mirror*, on Monday, 18th January 1904, records a 2-2 draw with East Midlands rivals Notts County as part of a round-up of what the newspaper describes as the "principal Association football matches", which had taken place two days earlier.

BELOW: The oldest surviving picture of Derby County in the *Mirror* ran on Monday, 10th October 1904, and showed action from the Rams' 3-2 victory over Bury the previous Saturday.

FOOTBALL.

The following were the results of the principal Association football matches on Saturday:—Middlesbrough (h) 2, West Bromwich Albion 2; Newcastle United (h) 1, Everton 0; Bury (h) 1, Sheffield Wednesday 0; Sheffield United (h) 1, Stoke 1; Liverpool (h) 2, Sunderland 1; Aston Villa (h) 1, Small Heath 1; Notts County 2, Derby County 2. Southern League: Tottenham Hotspur (h) 2, Queen's Park Rangers 2; West Ham United (h) 1, Plymouth Argyle 1; Swindon (h) 1, Brighton 1;

SATURDAY'S FOOTBALL.

1901 Steve Bloomer scores the 200th goal of his Derby career; only one man, Kevin Hector, has hit that milestone since. 1903 The FA Cup is becoming a heartbreaking competition for the club with another final defeat, 6-0 by Bury. 1905–06 The whole county is rocked by the news that Bloomer has been sold to Middlesbrough. 1907 Derby are relegated under the management of former player Jimmy Methven. 1909–10 Alf Bentley becomes the first player to score 30 goals in one season for the Rams. 1910 Bloomer's back from Boro: at 35, he returns to the fold and marks his second coming with two goals in a 5-0 victory over Lincoln. 1912 Promotion back to the First Division is attained thanks in no small part to the 18 goals scored by Bloomer. 1913 Ernald Scattergood becomes the first and only goalkeeper to score for the club with a penalty against Manchester City on the last day of the season. 1914 Life in the top flight is short-lived, with relegation back to the Second Division. 1915 The Rams claim the title to bounce straight back before the league is suspended following the start of the First World War.

–LEGENDS–

Steve Bloomer

As anyone who has visited Pride Park will know, Steve Bloomer's spirit lives on in Derby. The current crop of Rams are greeted at every home game with "Steve Bloomer's Watchin'", the annoyingly catchy ditty which serves as a reminder that the club's former players will always be remembered and appreciated by those supporters who came along well after they had last kicked a football. Bloomer is often referred to as the greatest player to have pulled on a Derby County shirt and, while such matters will always be subjective, there can be no argument that he was the club's first real hero. Bloomer was a terrific goalscorer and only two Englishmen, Jimmy Greaves and Dixie Dean, have scored more league goals at the top level than the Derby great. Bloomer finished top of the league scoring charts five times between 1896 and 1904, and was the club's top scorer for 13 consecutive seasons.

He formed a wonderful relationship with John Goodall at Derby and would always credit his team-mate with being the master to his pupil. Goodall was the top scorer in the Football League's inaugural season, his goals firing Preston North End to the Double before Derby snapped him up. In 1906, Bloomer was sold to Middlesbrough because of Derby's financial problems but he returned four years later. His international record was second to none as well. He scored in his first 10 appearances for England and averaged more than a goal a game for his country, failing to score in only five of his 23 matches. For a long time, Bloomer held the record for number of caps won. He played his last game for Derby in 1914, 11 days after turning 40, and then had a successful career as a coach in Germany, Spain and Holland before returning to his homeland. He later coached Derby's reserves and worked as a general assistant at the club. A bust of Bloomer was unveiled at Pride Park in 2009.

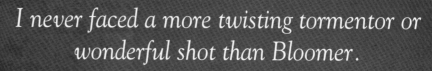

> *" I never faced a more twisting tormentor or wonderful shot than Bloomer.*
>
> Ernest Needham, Bloomer's England captain *"*

FOOTBALL
–STATS–

Steve Bloomer

Name: Stephen Bloomer

Born: 20th January 1874 (Cradley)

Died: 16th April 1938; aged 64

Playing career: Derby County, Middlesbrough, Derby County

Position: Inside-forward

Derby appearances: 525 (1892–1906 and 1910–14)

Derby goals: 332

England appearances: 23

England goals: 28

> *" The greater the match, the better he played.*
>
> Former FA secretary Frederick Wall *"*

BRILLIANT FOOTBALL AT PLUMSTEAD.

League Leaders' Third Defeat—Bury Win at Last— The 'Spurs Themselves Again—Corinthians Outclassed—Malvernians Triumph.

NOTES ON ALL THE LEADING GAMES.

Although there were no F.A. Cup-ties decided on Saturday, it was one of the busiest days in this eventful season. Whilst there were some sensational results, however, in the various games, in the majority of cases comparative form worked out fairly well. The game of the day, so far as London and the south was concerned, was undoubtedly that at Plumstead, which was witnessed by upwards of 35,000 spectators. In addition to this match, there was also a huge crowd at Park Royal, and at Upton Park, Brentford, Leyton, Richmond, and Blackheath the attendances were all above the average.

* * *

In the provinces the biggest gates were at Newcastle, where 27,000 people were present; Derby, Everton, Small Heath, Sheffield, Stoke, Bolton, Reading and Plymouth, in each case 10,000 or more spectators setting the turnstiles clicking to a merry tune. It was a delightful day for football, and this, added to the peculiar interest of some of the games, doubtless accounted for the big attendances.

* * *

* * *

Sheffield Wednesday are going through an altogether unusual experience for them. The champions met with their third successive defeat at Derby, the County beating them by 1 goal to 0. It was to weak forward play, maybe, that Wednesday owed their defeat, several very easy chances being missed by bad shooting. Malloch and Wilson perhaps were the greatest sinners in this respect. The back play of Morris and Methven, for Derby, and Layton and Burton, for Sheffield, was superb. The best half-back on the field was Ruddlesdin, who was making a reappearance for the Wednesday. The veteran proved one of the best stoppers that young Hounsfield the Derby amateur outside right, has met this season.

* * *

POSITION OF THE CLUBS.

The figures in parentheses denote the positions at the close of last season.

	Played	Won	Lost	Drn	Goals. For	Agst	Pts
Sunderland (6)	11	6	2	3	22	12	15
Preston North End	12	6	3	3	16	14	15
Sheffield Wed. (1)	10	7	3	0	20	11	14
Everton (3)	11	7	4	0	19	12	14
Sheffield United (7)	11	6	3	2	18	15	14
Derby County (14)	11	6	3	2	16	14	14
Newcastle United (4)	10	5	3	2	17	9	12
Small Heath (11)	10	5	4	1	18	12	11
Manchester City (2)	8	4	2	2	16	9	10
Blackburn R. (15)	10	4	4	2	16	12	10
Woolwich Arsenal	10	3	3	4	8	9	10
Wolverhampton W. (8)	10	5	5	0	16	18	10
Aston Villa (5)	11	4	6	1	15	18	9
Stoke (16)	11	4	6	1	8	19	9
Middlesbrough (10)	10	2	6	2	8	15	6
Notts Forest (9)	11	3	8	0	18	26	6
Notts County (13)	11	2	7	2	9	21	6
Bury (12)	10	1	8	1	10	28	3

Around the time the *Mirror* celebrated its first anniversary, the newspaper's football coverage remained at a premium – nothing like the multiple pages we are used to these days. Page 14 of the paper on 7th November 1904 provided a round-up of the action, which was the norm back then, with one paragraph given to each of the leading games. Derby's 10,000-plus crowd on what was described as a "delightful day for football" received an honourable mention, and the report of their 1-0 victory over reigning champions Sheffield Wednesday praised performances from Rams defenders Charlie Morris and Jimmy Methven, and young outside-right Reginald Hounsfield. As the table, which ran on the same page, showed, Derby sat sixth in the First Division that day, although they would go on to finish the campaign 11th out of 18 teams.

BLOOMER AND BRAWN JOIN MIDDLESBROUGH.

To-day's Important Football Matches—Two Internationals and League Fixtures.

PROSPECTS OF THE TEAMS.

BY CITIZEN.

To-day's list of football fixtures includes two international matches—England v. Scotland, at Edinburgh, under the Rugby code, and Scotland v. Ireland, at Dublin, at "Soccer." There is also a full list of League matches, and some of them are very important.

* * *

The League matches were fully dealt with by "Throstle" yesterday, and call for no further comment from me to-day. The international "Soccer" match between Ireland and Scotland is an interesting one from the fact that the Scots were beaten by Wales. Of late years Ireland have held their own with Scotland, beating them at Glasgow in 1903, drawing at Dublin in 1904, and losing at Glasgow last year. Ireland are not quite at full strength to-day, but they will give their opponents a good game.

In spite of Scotland's splendid reputation this season there is no question that England will put up a good game in the Rugby match at Inverleith this afternoon. The fight for the Calcutta Cup is always more or less one of most concern to the forwards. Chances of scoring are traditionally few, and so it behoves the sides to be keenly on the alert. Had fortune been completely equitable Scotland should now be in possession of victories against Wales and New Zealand; but her luck was dead out in both those matches.

England in their revised condition are a stronger combination than played in either of the other matches, and young Birkett's debut is one of the most interesting things connected with the fixture. Birkett's father and uncle were famous twenty-five years ago in football. And the genius seems to have been transmitted to J. G. G. Four years have passed since England held the Calcutta Cup.

* * *

In town Woolwich Arsenal play Derby County, and on recent form should still further improve their position in the League by a victory. The County will be without Bloomer, who has represented the club since 1892 and holds the record number of international caps. Derby people will learn this morning with a gasp of surprise that Bloomer has been transferred to Middlesbrough in order

STEVE BLOOMER.

to help pull the Teesiders out of the trouble they are in. He will turn out for them to-day at Liverpool. They have also secured Brawn, of Aston Villa, but it is doubtful whether the latter will be eligible this week. It is anticipated that the fees for these two transfers exceed £1,000.

* * *

In the Southern League there are two matches in town. An attractive game will be played at Tottenham, where the 'Spurs are opposing their old rivals, Millwall, who may win. Swindon visit Brentford, who are in such good form just now that they are nearly sure to capture both points. Fulham, the prospective champions, should win at Watford, and Southampton will probably take both points from Bristol Rovers at the Dell. The other matches have no bearing on the championship, but will be found in our fixture table.

* * *

There is a series of fine amateur matches in London this afternoon. The Corinthians have whipped up a good side to play Northampton at Queen's Club, though it is not representative, owing to the clashing with the London and Dunn Cups. If the Old Carthusians beat Old Aldenhamians they will meet Old Reptonians in the final for the latter competition. Old Malvernians v. New Crusaders and Casuals v. Dulwich Hamlet furnish two superb fixtures for the London Senior semi-finals. The Malvernians at full strength should beat the New Crusaders.

The news to which Derby fans woke on 17th March 1906 was not good: club hero Steve Bloomer had been sold to Middlesbrough, for £750. Bloomer was 32 and considered to be nearing the end of his career but, even so, the decision caused an outcry locally as he remained the heartbeat of the team. A year later, Derby were relegated to the Second Division and the pictures from the *Mirror* on 5th October 1908 show a trip to Tottenham, where the two sides played out a 0-0 league draw. Derby keeper Harry Maskrey was Man of the Match for the visitors, and is shown twice thwarting Spurs attacks.

DERBY COUNTY'S GOAL IN PERIL DURING SECOND LEAGUE MATCH WITH TOTTENHAM HOTSPUR.

A fast and exciting Second League game between Tottenham Hotspur and Derby County, on the former's ground, resulted on Saturday in a pointless draw. Chief credit for this result is due to Maskrey, the Derby goalkeeper, who time after time repelled the attack of the 'Spurs' forwards. Bevan, the visiting centre-forward, was injured in the first minute of the game, and could not reappear until after the interval. (1) A hot attack repelled by Maskrey. (2) Maskrey punches out the ball.

–LEGENDS–

Alf Bentley

Local lad Alf's reward for turning professional in 1906 was a £50 fee from the club. He finished the 1908–09 season top scorer in the Second Division, and two years later Bolton splashed out £1,000 to sign him. After two seasons in the northwest, Bentley moved to West Bromwich Albion for £500, and spent nine years at The Hawthorns before returning to hometown club Alfreton.

FOOTBALL –STATS–
Alf Bentley

Name: Alfred Bentley

Born: 15th September 1887 (Alfreton)

Died: 15th April 1940; aged 52

Playing career: Derby County, Bolton, West Brom, Burton, Alfreton

Position: Centre-forward

Derby appearances: 168 (1906–10)

Derby goals: 112

DERBY COUNTY IN THE SEMI-FINAL.

BENTLEY SCORES THREE GOALS AGAINST THE FOREST

By beating Notts Forest at Derby by 3 goals to nil in the postponed English Cup-tie Derby County again enter the semi-final. All three goals were scored by Bentley, Derby's centre forward. The picture shows Scattergood (Derby) clearing.—(*Daily Mirror* photograph.)

–LEGENDS–

Ernald Scattergood

Ernald Scattergood wrote his name into the history books in 1913 when he became the first Derby goalkeeper to score a penalty for the club, slotting home from the spot against Manchester City. He repeated the feat on two more occasions – both times from the penalty spot – and, almost a century later, remains the only No 1 to have scored for the Rams. Scattergood, who had the wonderful middle name 'Oak', made just one appearance for England – a 4-3 victory over Wales at Bristol City's Ashton Gate on 17th March 1913 in the Home Championship tournament.

FOOTBALL –STATS–
Ernald Scattergood

Name: Ernald Oak Scattergood

Born: 29th May 1887 (Riddings)

Died: 2nd July 1932; aged 45

Playing career: Derby County

Position: Goalkeeper

Derby appearances: 192 (1906–14)

Derby goals: 3

England appearances: 1

Mr. Frank Buckley, the noted Derby County football player, is a farmer when not at play. He is an expert agriculturist, and perhaps his football battles derive some of their vigour from his active life on the farm. Mr. Buckley does his training for the football season on his farm, where he has an up-to-date gymnasium.

(1) Mr. Buckley training on rowing machine in his gymnasium at Redditch, Worcestershire. (2) With his horses. (3) Mr. Buckley sprinting. He finds that a long run in the country air is the best of training. (4) With his sheep.—(*Daily Mirror* photographs.)

ABOVE: Disgruntled fans have no doubt used the word agricultural to describe a fair few Derby performances down the years, but Frank Buckley put an entirely different spin on it during his season at the club between 1913 and 1914. On 25th September 1913 the *Mirror* carried a lovely sequence of pictures showing half-back Buckley at home on his farm, putting in some extra training and tending to his animals.

RIGHT: The front page of the *Mirror* on Monday, 17th November 1913, shows action from Derby's goalless draw at Chelsea two days earlier. Ernald Scattergood was largely responsible for keeping Chelsea at bay that day and is pictured claiming another ball into the box.

Chelsea v. Derby County at Chelsea. Scattergood, the Derby goalkeeper, saving a hard shot in the match, won by Chelsea by 2 to 1.

Derby County v. Aston Villa on a snow-covered ground at Derby.

ABOVE: There was no such thing as undersoil heating at football stadiums in the early 1900s, so it will come as no surprise that the FA Cup first-round tie between Derby and Aston Villa at the Baseball Ground on Saturday, 11th January 1913, didn't reach a conclusion. The match was replayed four days later, with Villa winning 3-1.

CUP-TIES UNCOMPLETED.

ilizzard caused the game to be abandoned.

BELOW: They really don't make 'em like they used to: while bobble hats, scarves, snoods and earmuffs are worn to keep even the slightest of chills off in modern times, flat caps sufficed as the snow fell in Derby back at the start of 1913. As the caption reveals, half of the 32 FA Cup ties held that Saturday had to be abandoned because of the bleak midwinter conditions.

Crowd watching the game between Derby County and Aston Villa in a driving snowstorm.

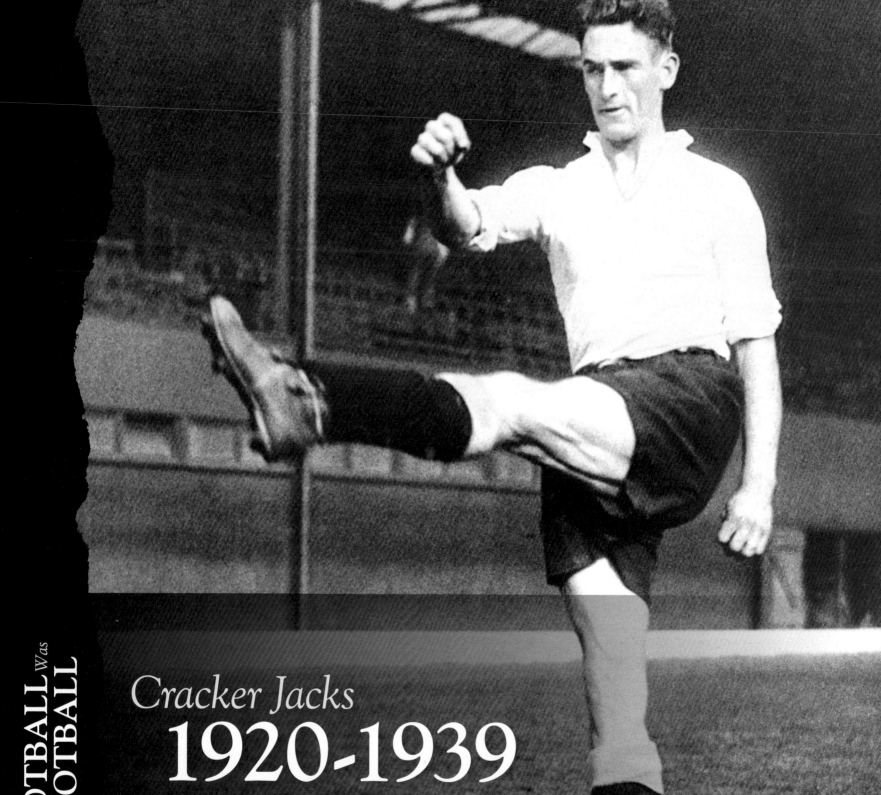

Cracker Jacks
1920-1939

Jack Nicholas (right) and Jack Bowers (left) were hugely important members of the first team before the Second World War. Nicholas missed only four of Derby's 356 games – three in the league and one in the FA Cup – in eight years from 1931 to 1939, and remains the second longest-serving player in the club's history, behind Sammy Crooks. In total, Nicholas spent 18 years and 100 days on the playing staff, while Crooks' record of 19 years and 18 days is unlikely to be beaten. Nicholas' nickname on the Pop Side during his later days with the club was *Owd Nick* – that's *Old Nick* to those of you who grew up outside Derbyshire – and it proved quite apt given that he joined Derby Borough Police Force after hanging up his boots. Bowers, meanwhile, was prolific in front of goal and twice battered his way into the club's record books with his tallies for a season. Bowers scored 183 times for Derby, 167 goals coming in the league and 16 in the FA Cup.

> *Jack [Nicholas] was a smashing fellow to get on with. He was stern and all the rest of it. In fact when I went from Chesterfield to Derby, he didn't speak to me for quite some time. I went to play right-half … Jack felt I was going to shove him out, but they moved him to right-back and it wasn't until he'd played right-back for a bit that he started talking to me.*
>
> Jimmy Bullions

1921 Relegation back to the Second Division. **1922** After 31 years as a player and then manager, Jimmy Methven, who made 511 appearances for Derby, departs the club. Cecil Potter replaces him. **1924** Derby County buy the Baseball Ground from Francis Ley. **1925** George Jobey replaces Potter and the club wins promotion back to the First Division. The new main stand on Shaftesbury Crescent is opened. **1929–30** The Rams finish second in the First Division. **1930–31** Jack Bowers blasts 37 league goals, 39 in total, to smash his own goalscoring record. **1932** Jack Nicholas begins a run of games which will see him play 328 out of 331 in the league, up until the end of the 1938–39 campaign. **1932–33** The prolific Bowers breaks his own record again with an astonishing 43 goals in one season. **1933–34** A double-decker stand is added to the Baseball Ground at the Osmaston Road end. **1934–35** The Normanton end stand is opened. **1939–45** League football is suspended following the outbreak of the Second World War.

The Twenties did not start well for Derby, with the club relegated to the Second Division in 1921, and the following year manager Jimmy Methven, 31 years after joining the Rams as a player, departing. He was replaced by Cecil Potter, who, after finishing 14th in his first season, twice missed out on promotion by one place, finishing third in the 1923–24 and 1924–25 campaigns before he, too, was replaced, by George Jobey. Where Potter narrowly failed, Jobey succeeded, and in his first season in charge he led the Rams back to the top flight. Jobey spent 16 years at the Baseball Ground and twice led the club to the runners-up spot in the First Division. In 1941, however, his world caved in when he and four directors – alderman H G Pattison, Bendle W Moore, H T Ann and Ben Robshaw – were handed life bans by the Football Association after a disciplinary panel found them guilty of making illegal payments. Former director O J Jackson was also permanently suspended, while another ex-director, A Green, was suspended for three years, and the club was fined £500. Jobey's ban was lifted in 1945, but he only spent one more season in football, as manager of Mansfield Town in 1952–53.

Putting Backs Into It

EVER since the days of Tom Cooper and George Collin the public of Derby have been crying out at Derby County, "Your backs aren't a patch on the old pair." Nobody knows that better than manager George Jobey.

"What the public don't realise," he says, "is that it takes three or four years to produce a pair with the same understanding and ability."

But George Jobey thinks that he is now well on the way to producing another back division of the old calibre. He has a pair in Wilcox and Alton, whom he claims will develop the same sound combination.

And the way he's doing it is by switching them over into reverse positions every three or four weeks Equips them all round, that system.

George Jobey was blessed with two fine full-backs in Tom Cooper and George Collin during his early years as Derby manager but, after their departures, he occasionally had to use the print media to remind Rams fans that their replacements, George Wilcox and Thomas Alton, would need time to reach the same levels.

ABOVE: The *Mirror* records the downfall of Jobey and Derby's directors at the hands of a Football Association disciplinary committee on Friday, 29th August 1941.

BELOW: Derby signed goalscorer Dai Astley from Aston Villa in 1936, and his goals helped the club finish fourth in his first season. The following year, the Rams disappointingly finished in mid-table and, during the following season, Astley joined Blackpool. The Tangerines weren't the first club to talk to Astley about taking him from Derby that term, either, as the *Mirror* reported on Monday, 27th October 1938.

–LEGENDS–

Jack Bowers

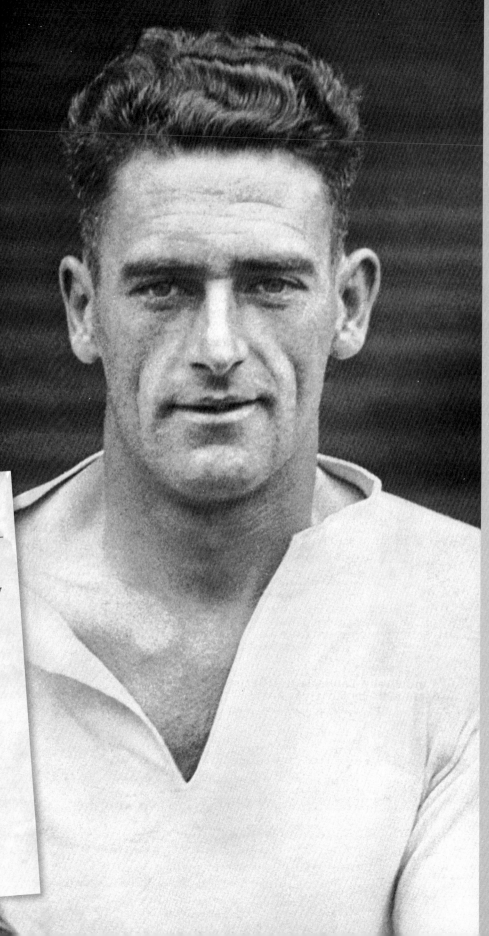

Bowers' goals-to-games ratio was quite extraordinary. He was prolific for Derby, and only Steve Bloomer and Kevin Hector have scored more times for the club. Bowers, who went on to be the club's physio after he had hung up his boots, set the club record for the most league goals scored in a season – 37 in 33 games – in 1930–31, hitting 39 in total, and two years later he fired home an astonishing 43 in all competitions. He won his first England cap against Ireland in the 1934 British Home Championship, scoring on his debut, and played against Wales and Scotland in the same competition, scoring against the latter. His son John made 65 appearances for Derby between 1957 and 1966.

FOOTBALL –STATS–

Jack Bowers

Name: John William Anslow Bowers

Born: 22nd February 1908 (Scunthorpe)

Died: 4th July 1970; aged 62

Playing career: Derby County, Leicester City

Position: Centre-forward

Derby appearances: 220 (1928–36)

Derby goals: 183

England appearances: 3

England goals: 2

ENGLAND'S YOUNG MEN BEAT IRISH LEAGUE

BOWERS STARS IN VICTORY
BY FOUR CLEAR GOALS

Visitors Fade Out After Bright Start—Attack of Many Ideas and Great Speed

BY A SPECIAL CORRESPONDENT

The Football League's decision to give youth its chance in the first representative English side of the season was brilliantly justified in the game with the Irish League at Preston yesterday, when England won 4—0.

After an undistinguished opening, the side, which contained a defence and half-back line new to this class of match, became splendidly balanced and brimful of confidence.

The Irishmen, who have never yet beaten the English League, were fortunate to get off with the loss of only four goals.

England's inability to settle down in the first twenty minutes may be attributed in no small measure to the deep "W" formation in attack, which prevented the inside men from finding their colleagues easily with their passes.

BASTIN A ROVER

Bastin played as a go-between twixt Allen, at centre half, and Bowers, the leader of the attack, and his colleagues were some time getting accustomed to his roving style.

He had three shots in the first quarter of an hour, but poor ones.

In the last fifteen minutes before the interval he showed the line a splendid example and the game quickly turned in the Englishmen's favour.

Crooks, the captain, had been England's best forward, and he made the centre from which Bowers headed the opening goal, though it was Bastin and Brook who framed the move.

The turning point in the game was the second goal, secured from a penalty kick which seemed to be unjustified, for although Charlton brought Bowers down heavily his charge appeared to be as clean as it was vigorous.

Before this goal the Irishmen had been twice unlucky not to score through Martin, who, on the second occasion, shot on the wrong side of an empty goal after beating the whole defence.

Even worse luck attended the Irishmen's efforts just after the interval. Shearer struck the post and saw the ball travel across the goal before Sagar could scoop it away.

MEN OF THE MATCH

The goals in the second half were from headers by Crooks and Bowers. The latter's second success set the seal on his all-round qualities of leadership of an attack that was full of ideas and pace.

The Irish forwards, after a bright opening in which the inside men, Shearer and Coulter, spoon-fed Martin, gradually faded out.

Copping, of Leeds, left half, was the most consistent of the English half-backs, but Allen, of Portsmouth, at centre half, was a big power in attack.

The defence was sound, but never brilliant, and the chief success was that of the attack, in which Bastin, Brook, Bowers and Crooks were the men of the match.

Martin, the nineteen-year-old Irish centre forward from Belfast Celtic, whose transfer has been sought by Huddersfield and Everton, looked a mere stripling, but he had sound football ideas.

Pinkerton in goal was the Irishmen's hero.

Bowers (Derby County).

Bowers' goalscoring exploits for Derby regularly made headline news in the *Mirror*, with four goals in a 6-2 league win over Chelsea in December 1930 and two against Wolves in a 3-0 FA Cup third-round victory in 1934 earning him special mentions. The Derby man also shone when he was picked for a Football League representative XI to face an Irish League XI in 1933.

West Ham Like Seaside Air—Chelsea Crumple at Derby

First League football provided another crop of goals and thrills on Saturday.

The Arsenal still lead, although their game with Grimsby was abandoned through fog. Several teams won away, including the Wednesday, who inflicted the first home defeat upon Portsmouth.

Sunderland just beat Liverpool by 6 goals to 5, and Derby County upset Chelsea's reorganised team by 6 goals to 2.

Bowers, Derby's new centre forward, was the individual star with four goals to his credit. The Villa, West Ham and Middlesbrough all secured smart away victories.

SCORING REVELS

Eleven Goals at Sunderland—Bowers Upsets Chelsea

WOLVES FIND THE RAMS UNAFRAID

Derby on Top of Form at the Baseball Ground

BY A SPECIAL CORRESPONDENT

Like an audience before a conjurer, Derby County supporters saw on Saturday a feat performed that at one time seemed impossible.

There had been during the week scares regarding injured players, but the air of mystery was cleared a few minutes before the match started.

Then the record crowd of over 37,000 at the Baseball Ground saw that the only Derby absentee was Ramage.

As foreshadowed, Wileman deputised, and was prominent always in an attacking line that ran up three unanswered goals.

Despite some Wolverhampton shock tactics, the match was never in doubt, and in the first half Derby showed themselves potential League champions and Cupholders in one.

Two minutes from the start Jack Bowers once more showed himself the opportunist he is, and when the ball rebounded from the upright from Groves, Bowers tapped it past Wildman.

Twenty minutes later Bowers scored again, through the brilliance of Duncan, who pulled back the ball from the goal-line and put across a perfect centre.

KIRBY'S BRILLIANCE

This time it was Bowers's head which did the trick. It was a typical Bowers-Duncan goal.

The Wolves howled round Derby's goal several times, but found the Rams anything but tender meat.

Once Goddard raced through, passed Barker and defeated Cooper's challenge, but Kirby took the ball off his foot.

The County made trebly sure of the fifth round in the second half. This time it was Crooks who scored with a header.

The winger had been well policed, but he slipped through a trap to accept a deliberately placed shot from Duncan.

The Wolves never looked like winners, although it must be said in fairness that they found Derby on the very top of their form.

During the second half the Wolves tried to ginger up the attack by changing over Phillips and Beattie on the right wing, but their sharpshooters found Kirby in goal coolness personified.

For instance, in the last kick of the match Beattie shot point blank, but found Kirby's hands were waiting calmly for it.

" *Jack is a club legend. He was a good footballer and a lovely man.* "

Roy McFarland

From Wembley to Workington
1946-1966

Captain Jack Nicholas shows off the FA Cup as he and his team-mates embark on an open-top bus tour of Derby following their 4-1 triumph over Charlton at Wembley in May 1946.

> *Right from the start, I never had any doubts that we were going to win.*
>
> Raich Carter on the 1946 FA Cup final

1946 The FA Cup hoodoo is no more as Derby beat Charlton 4-1 after extra-time to finally lift the trophy. **1947** The club pays a British record transfer fee to sign Billy Steel from Greenock Morton. **1949** The big spenders splash out again, snapping up Johnny Morris from Manchester United for another British record fee. **1953** The club is hit by relegation to the Second Division and, that November, with the Rams struggling, manager Stuart McMillan is sacked and replaced by Jack Barker. **1955** Yet another relegation sends the club into the Third Division (North) for the first time. **1957** Derby, now under Harry Storer, win the title. **1962–63** Tim Ward takes over as manager and his arrival coincides with the emergence of full-back Ron Webster and the signing of midfielder Alan Durban; Jack Parry and Geoff Barrowcliffe become the fourth and fifth players to chalk up 500 games for the club. **1966** Derby break their own transfer record to sign 21-year-old Kevin Hector from Bradford Park Avenue.

–LEGENDS–

Raich Carter

After scoring 121 goals in 248 games for Sunderland, Carter moved to Derby – for whom he had guested during the Second World War – in 1945, and struck up a partnership with Peter Doherty which would play a huge part in the Rams winning the FA Cup a year later. That victory meant Carter was the only person to have picked up winners' medals before and after the war. Despite turning out only 63 times for Derby, the role Carter played in that triumph at Wembley, and, indeed, the build-up to it, endeared him to the Rams faithful, who quickly realized what a special player he was.

FOOTBALL –STATS–

Raich Carter

Name: Horatio Stratton Carter
Born: 21st December 1913 (Hendon)
Died: 9th October 1994; aged 80
Playing career: Sunderland, Derby County, Hull
Position: Inside-forward
Managerial career: Hull, Leeds, Mansfield, Middlesbrough
Derby appearances: 63 (1945–48)
Derby goals: 34
England appearances 13
England goals: 7

THEY KEPT BAD NEWS FROM HIM WHILE HE HELPED DERBY WIN THE CUP

The King shaking hands with Horatio Carter at the Cup Final at Wembley on Saturday.

RUNNING from the Wembley pitch with his Cup medal in his hands, grey-haired Horatio (Raich) Carter, hero of Derby County's Cup Final win, was met by a club official, who pulling him aside, quietly said, "I'm sorry Raich, I've had news."

Then, while the cheering of the crowd echoed through the dressing-room, Carter heard that his father-in-law, the man who was behind his transfer from Sunderland to Derby County, had died an hour before the game.

He was Mr. Edgar Marsh, with whom Carter and his wife had been living in Chaddesden, near Derby, since they were bombed out of their Sunderland home.

A telephone message telling of Mr. Marsh's death was sent to Wembley where Mrs. Carter was watching her husband play, but it was decided not to tell Carter until after the game.

As the players' motor-coach was leaving Wembley Stadium the Cup winners were singing.

Carter told his team mates the news. The singing stopped, but outside the cheers went on.

2 KILLED, 40 HURT IN GERMAN TOWN RIOT

Rioting broke out yesterday in the German town of Diessen, near Landsberg, in the U.S. zone, between 5,000 Jewish displaced persons and German civilians.

Two people were killed and forty injured and a 7 p.m. to 5 a.m. curfew was imposed.

ABOVE: Derby's FA Cup final victory was tinged with sadness for Carter, and two days later the *Mirror* explained why.

The Road to Wembley

Que sera, sera, whatever will be, will be, we're going to Wem-ber-lee … How the Rams arrived at the Twin Towers:

Third round:
Luton 0 Derby 6 (5th January 1946);
Derby 3 Luton 0 (9th January 1946).
Derby win 9-0 on aggregate.

Fourth round:
Derby 1 West Bromwich Albion 0 (26th January 1946);
West Bromwich Albion 1 Derby 3 (30th January 1946).
Derby win 4-1 on aggregate.

Fifth round:
Brighton 1 Derby 4 (9th February 1946);
Derby 6 Brighton 0 (14th February 1946).
Derby win 10-1 on aggregate.

Quarter-finals:
Aston Villa 3 Derby 4 (2nd March 1946);
Derby 1 Aston Villa 1 (6th March 1946).
Derby win 5-4 on aggregate.

Semi-finals:
Derby 1 Birmingham City 1 (23rd March 1946).

Replay:
Birmingham City 0 Derby 4 (27th March 1946).

FINAL TEAMS

DERBY: Woodley, Nicholas, Howe, Bullions, Leuty, Musson, Harrison, Carter, Stamps, Doherty, Duncan.

CHARLTON: Bartram, Phipps, Shreeve, H Turner, Oakes, Johnson, Fell, Brown, A Turner, Welsh, Duffy.

REF: E D Smith (Whitehaven).

ATTENDANCE: 98,215.

Sports Mirror

THIS, THEN, IS CUP DAY—

John Thompson's Sportfolios

Jack Nicholas, Derby captain: "We are all confident we will win."

Don Welsh, opposite number: "The soft ground will help us."

In the desert and across Europe and in the jungle during the long years that are over the singular magic of our greatest game was a constant star....

IN the orchards of Normandy and sand-swept camps of Libya, the talk came always to memories of football's greatest day...

Of the tension and tradition which lift the final game of the F.A. Cup into something considerably more than the spectacle of twenty-two young men kicking a football around on a green field at Wembley.

And this, then is Cup Final Day, the first since war ended.

LET us commiserate with all who will not be there—and with three who will be there but not playing: Charlton's Peter Croker, Derby County's Jack Parr and Samuel Crooks, stalwarts who helped their teams into the Final—and then lost their chance of the precious gold medal through injury.

For nineteen years, man and boy, Crooks, at outside-right, has been an inspiration to his colleagues and a worry to the opposition. Now he is in his last season of active football.

INTO Crooks's shoes steps Reginald Harrison, 22, a Derby native who worked his way up the football grade with the Derby boys' team; by trade a painter and decorator; by profession a devoted follower of the Crooks style and manner.

Ever since his injury in the sixth round, Sammy Crooks has been coaching the boy who is now to take his place; showing him the tricks that fool an opponent, warning him against the trick too many.

No greater testimony than this could be paid to any man's team spirit.

A FEW weeks back from Burma, left-back John Howe, music-loving steelworker, was mixing himself a last tonic (raw egg in sherry) when I called at County's hotel yesterday.

In the lounge, Mrs. Ben Robshaw, wife of Derby's chairman, was busy with needle and thread sewing up a black and white doll which supporters had sent as a mascot.

Players cheered when she presented it to tough, burly John Nicholas, their captain, who rocked it in his arms, chanted "Bring us luck, baby."

Only worry in the camp was caused by players wondering whether it would rain—the tickets issued for their wives were marked "Not under cover."

Rival manager Jimmy Seed came to the rescue after a phone call from Derby's Stuart McMillan. *Now rain or fine the wives will watch in comfort*

MOST of the Derby players have other jobs to occupy their minds. There is flame-headed Peter Doherty, a builder on the field and off; Bullions and Stamps, the miners; Leuty, the machine tool maker; Musson, the moulder; Nicholas, who joined the club at sixteen, and became a policeman during the war.

Not forgetting possibly the greatest inside forward of his day, Horatio Carter, the grey- head, twenty times capped by his country

DERBY GET THE VOTE

IT is in their forward line that Charlton's strength lies: Leslie Fell and Chris Duffy, the wingers; Albert Brown, the funny man of the party, and Donald Welsh, the captain, who emerged yesterday from a slight motor-car accident as unruffled as usual; and Arthur Turner, who revels in a heavy ground, to spearhead the attack.

Turner, Coastal Command bomb-aimer, was fished out of the sea after his machine had crashed. Little could he have dreamed as he waited for rescue of this day at Wembley.

WHAT of prospects? In a toss-up game in which anything can happen and in which more goals can be expected than in most finals, my fancy is for Derby.

Reason: With most departments equal in talent I think that the exceptional brilliance of Derby's inside forwards will tip the balance.

Manager Seed's last words: "May the best team win. I hope it will be Charlton...."

And Manager McMillan's: "I think it will be Derby's Cup...."

I believe today in Mr McMillan as a prophet.

How the Mirror covered FA Cup final day

Derby fans hoping to see pictures of their side winning the FA Cup for the first time would have been disappointed with the coverage in the *Sunday Pictorial* – later to become the *Sunday Mirror* – the following day. A London bias? Perhaps. This was the front page of the paper and it showed Charlton's despair at the own goal which gave the Rams their first lead, rather than the East Midlanders' joy. Page 3 at least shows Derby skipper Jack Nicholas being hoisted onto the shoulders of a team-mate, with the famous old trophy firmly in his grasp.

There is agony written on the face of this footballer. He is Shreeve, the Charlton full back, and you see him watching the ball go into the net off the boot of his colleague Turner—to give Derby County their first goal that led to their smashing Cup win at Wembley. Turner, even more horrified, lies beside him on the ground.

The double signing of inside-forwards Raich Carter and Peter Doherty, both of whom had guested for the club during the war years, meant Derby had a strong team for their first final since 1903, but still the first goal of the game did not arrive until the 85th minute, when Bert Turner deflected Dally Duncan's shot past his own keeper to give the Rams the lead. A minute later, however, Turner levelled matters with a goal at the right end to force extra-time. While normal time might have been close, Derby stepped it up in the extra period, with Doherty scoring early to regain the lead and Jack Stamps then striking twice to give Derby a 4-1 victory, which saw them crowned FA Cup winners for the first time.

SUNDAY PICTORIAL, April 28, 1946

Sunday Pictorial

THE MAN WHO WALKED AWAY

"I Foresaw Bad Luck Because No. 13 Was Our Room Number"

BY STANLEY RUSSELL

IN silence, Jimmy Seed, manager of Charlton, watched as the King gave the F.A. Cup to his rivals, Derby County, at Wembley yesterday. Then he walked away.

His disappointment showed on his face, and he went on to the dressing rooms, a solitary figure, recognising none of his friends who offered him sympathy.

In the Charlton dressing room later, Jimmy Seed told me: "I had a foreboding about this game. This is the second time we have been in the unlucky dressing room at Wembley (its number was 13), and the second time we have been beaten.

"The only other time we have played here we had the lucky room—and we won.

"As for this match—well, the better team won, but we had our chances in the first half hour. If we had taken them, the result might have confounded all these superstitions."

Jack Nicholas, the Derby captain, who was given the cup by the King, told me: "After the first ten minutes there was only one team in it. I have been telling everybody for a long time that we should win."

LONDONERS had to take a back seat in the West End last night while supporters of the winners—and losers—celebrated. They paraded singing, whirling their rattles and dancing.

If a regular in the West End wanted a drink he had to wait hopefully on the fringe of the crowd, hoping the barman would see him. Cafes and restaurants were crammed.

Motor coaches on their way home paraded the West End, their radiators decorated with replicas of the Cup.

IT was a golden half-mile yesterday for the ticket touts from Wembley Park Station to the Stadium.

Husky-voiced gentlemen muttered to the streaming crowds: "Any tickets for sale? Give you fifteen bob for a 3s. 6d. ticket, mister."

If you wanted to buy a 3s. 6d. ticket it cost you 30s.

Then the price went up to two guineas and £3.

One man who went to Wembley did not see the game, but came away nearly £500 richer. He was selling unofficial programmes—20,000 of them.

We've got it! Victorious Derby players carry their skipper aloft, and Jack Nicholas hardly seems able to believe his luck. He peeps inside the prized cup—probably in search of a quick one to toast his team mates.

AS for the crowds, there has never been a more orderly 93,000 people than the second biggest Cup Final crowd in history which filled Wembley Stadium.

Even the single little bit of potential trouble was dealt with swiftly, smoothly and efficiently

Coming home with the Cup

Derby's triumphant stars wind down with a game of cards on the journey home, while the emotion of the day took it out of trainer Dave Willis, who opted for a bit of shut-eye instead.

Thousands turned out in Derby on 1st May 1946 to see the FA Cup winners parade their silverware. Captain Jack Nicholas and his team-mates made their way slowly through the city's streets before displaying the Cup from a balcony at police headquarters.

–LEGENDS–

Jack Stamps

Jack Stamps was a strapping Yorkshireman who cemented his place in Derby folklore when he struck twice during extra-time in the FA Cup final against Charlton. A fine goalscorer with a powerful shot, he might have won the Cup final in normal time had the ball not burst when he struck it with the game tied at 1-1. George Jobey signed Stamps for £1,500 and the latter's debut was a real sign of things to come: he scored twice in a 3-1 home win against Charlton Athletic in the First Division on 18th March 1939. Stamps enlisted in the Royal Artillery and, in 1940, was one of the final few soldiers in the British Expeditionary Force to be evacuated from Dunkirk. He lost his sight in his 50s but that didn't stop him regularly attending Rams matches with his old mate, Maurice Hodgkin, a former Burton player, who would talk him through the action. Stamps became an honourary vice-president of the club in 1983. The Jack Stamps Trophy is awarded at the end of every season to the Player of the Year, as voted by Derby fans.

Jack Stamps in action against Wolves at the Baseball Ground on 8th October 1949. Derby lost 2-1, with Stamps scoring the Rams' goal.

FOOTBALL
–STATS–

Jack Stamps

Name: John David Stamps

Born: 2nd December 1918 (Thrybergh)

Died: 19th November 1991; aged 72

Playing career: Mansfield, Derby County, Shrewsbury

Position: Forward

Derby appearances: 262 (1938–53)

Derby goals: 126

Stamps Impresses

ANOTHER successful lad was eighteen-year-old Jack Stamps, hero of Derby County's win over Charlton.

He scored two goals, just missed two more, and was in the picture all through.

He gave both Duncan and McCulloch many useful passes and occasionally slung over nicely-placed long ones for Crooks on the right.

Derby stars pose for a team photo on 25th September 1947. They are (back row, left to right): Timothy Ward, Leon Leuty, Bert Mozley, William Townsend, Walter "Chick" Musson and Jack Howe. Front row, in kit, left to right: George Antonio, Frank Broome, Raich Carter, Billy Steel and Allen Oliver.

Record-breaking Rams

There was delight in Derby in 1947 when the club won the race for inside-left Billy Steel, beating off competition from several clubs, including Liverpool and Middlesbrough. It took a British record transfer fee of £15,500 to land the Scot. Steel wasn't always the most popular player in the Derby dressing room but there was no doubting his talent and, in 124 appearances for the club, he scored 35 goals. Two years later, the Rams were splashing the cash and breaking records again, this time for Johnny Morris from Manchester United, although, as the *Mirror* reported, the then-23-year-old's £24,500 move had to be sanctioned by the two women in his life.

Morris, pictured opposite left after signing for Derby, had won the FA Cup with United in 1948 and immediately began to repay the faith his new employers had shown in him, scoring 13 times in his first 13 games. He went on to score 47 goals in 140 games for Derby and made his England debut while at the Baseball Ground, before being sold to Leicester in 1952.

£15,000 player
Record fee for Billy Steel

BILLY STEEL, Great Britain and Greenock Morton inside left, was transferred yesterday to Derby County for the record fee of £15,000. Previous record was £14,000, paid by Arsenal for Bryn Jones in 1938.

The signing was made against competition from five English and two Scottish clubs.

As soon as the deal was completed in Glasgow, Mr. Stuart McMillan, County manager, hustled Steel and his fiancee into his car and drove them to Derby, where the player signed his contract.

"Steel was keen to come to Derby, because he played in several wartime games with two of our lads, Jack Howe and Tim Ward," said Derby chairman, Mr. Ben Robshaw. "We've managed to get him a house, and now he's going to get married and settle in Derby."

Ten years ago Steel, who is twenty-four, 5ft. 6in., and weighs 10½st., was a schoolboy international.

He was demobbed from the Army at the beginning of this year.

Liverpool and Middlesbrough were after him, but they backed out.

CHARLTON, too, signed a Scot, Alex McCrae, inside left, of Hearts. Fee is around £9,000, and a record for the Scottish club.

McCrae, a miner, is delighted with the move. "It will make a tremendous difference to me," he said, after the deal had been put through in Edinburgh. "It means just as much to my wife and our baby, and we are all looking forward to the change."

Billy Steel.

BABY HOLDS UP £25,000 SOCCER TRANSFER

A WORLD'S record football transfer was held up yesterday . . . by a baby a few hours old.

Derby County, offering a fee approaching £25,000, had received permission from Manchester United to see Johnny Morris, 23, United's inside forward on the transfer list.

Derby manager Stuart McMillan travelled to Manchester yesterday, but found that Morris would not go ahead with a move until he had talked it over with his wife Marion, who had just given birth to a daughter in Urmston (Manchester) Hospital.

Last night Johnny saw her—and the new arrival. And he announced to the waiting Soccer world: "My wife is going to sleep on it."

Derby, still in the First Division, line up for a team photo on 6th October 1951. They are (back row, left to right): Ken Oliver, Bert Mozley, Ray Middleton, Geoff Barrowcliffe, Colin Bell, Stephen McLachlan. Front row, from left to right: Reg Harrison, Johnny Morris, Jack Stamps, Jack Parry and Hugh McLaren.

A game against Newcastle on 1st November 1952 at St James' Park. On this occasion Ray Middleton punches clear under pressure from Toon striker Vic Keeble, but the Derby goalkeeper couldn't prevent the Magpies winning 1-0.

A change of manager at the Baseball Ground, which saw former player Jack Barker, who made 353 appearances for Derby, brought in to replace Stuart McMillan, prompted Jackie Stamps to leave the club and join up with his old team-mate Sammy Crooks, who had taken over as Shrewsbury manager. Stamps spoke to the *Mirror* on 18th December 1952 to explain his decision.

SOCCER: Policy change has wrecked his hope of job for life, he says

STAMPS QUITS DERBY — 'NO FUTURE'

"Daily Mirror" Reporter

WHILE a Soccer star of the past switched clubs yesterday in a bid for "security," a star of the future jumped from Division III into Division I—because of a fire.

The **STAR OF THE PAST**, thirty-five-year-old Jack Stamps, inside forward, moved from Derby County to Shrewsbury Town for a "small" fee.

Before this, he had turned down several transfer offers, thinking he was certain to stay with Derby when his playing days were over.

He said last night: "A little while ago there was a good chance that I would be certain of security at Derby.

"But then the change of management at the Baseball ground meant a reorganisation of the club's policy, and it was obvious that I could not be certain of getting the coaching and scouting job that I was hoping for."

"I have to think of my future, and I am convinced that my family and I will be comfortable and happy at Shrewsbury."

The signing was completed by Jack's former Derby team-mate, Sammy Crooks, now managing Shrewsbury.

The 'General'

"I wanted a 'general' to lead the side," said Sammy yesterday, "and in Stamps I think I have found one."

Jack will continue training at Derby until he moves with his family to a new house in Shrewsbury in the New Year.

The **STAR OF THE FUTURE**, twenty-three-year-old centre half or full back Geoff Twentyman, was signed from Carlisle United by Liverpool, who on Wednesday paid Watford £7,000 for goalkeeper David Underwood.

Needed Money

The cost of Liverpool's latest bid to strengthen their defence was not disclosed, but the fee is believed to be a five-figure one.

This is backed up by Carlisle's statement that they let Twentyman go only because they needed money after the destruction of their stand by fire earlier this year.

Manager Fred Emery said: "The destruction of the stand was a big loss. We have to build up our finances, so we had to let Geoff go."

Also in the transfer market yesterday were PLYMOUTH ARGYLE and CHESTER.

Argyle paid Luton about £5,000 for Hugh McJarrow, 25, inside or centre forward, formerly with Sheffield Wednesday and Chesterfield.

Chester signed Bernard Morrey, 25, outside right or left, from Newport County.

MEN ON THE MOVE

| STAMPS | TWENTYMAN | McJARROW |
| "Small ice" | Five-figures | £5,000 |

Derby were in the Second Division when Barker took over but, with the club relegated for the first time to the Third Division (North) at the end of his second season, where they faced such clubs as Workington AFC, he didn't last too long. The Rams then turned to Harry Storer. Derby were runners-up in his first season but won the league the following year to secure promotion back to the Second Division.

Newly appointed Derby manager Harry Storer (centre) on 4th August 1955 with new signings Martin McDonnell (left) and Paddy Ryan. Brian Clough was an admirer of Storer's no-nonsense style of management. Legend has it that one Monday morning Storer, who had played 270 times for the club in the Twenties and also played cricket for Derbyshire, called a player to join him at the Baseball Ground and told him to accompany him on a walk round the pitch. The manager's eyes were fixed firmly to the turf as the pair completed a full lap. Finally, the player discovered what this was all about. Storer told him: "I'm looking for that bloody hole you crawled into during Saturday's match."

–LEGENDS–

Jack Parry

A member of the Rams' 500 Club, Parry spent 17 years playing for his hometown team. A witty and popular member of the dressing room but a tenacious footballer as well, he made 483 league appearances for Derby – and only one of those was from the substitute's bench. He once had trainer Ralph Hann, himself a former player, in stitches when he ran on to treat him. Hann, fearing concussion, asked Parry if he knew where he was. "We're at Wembley," came the reply. "We're beating Brazil 2-0 and I've got 'em both." Parry's brother, Glyn, was also on Derby's books, while another brother, Ray, played for Bolton and England, and yet another, Cyril, for Notts County.

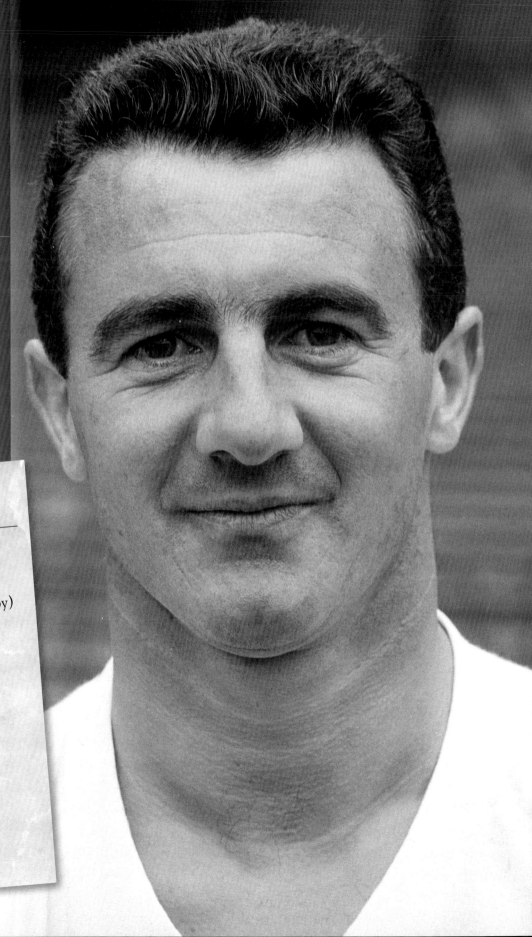

FOOTBALL –STATS–

Jack Parry

Name: Jack Parry

Born: 29th July 1931 (Derby)

Playing career: Derby County, Boston United

Position: Inside-forward

Derby appearances: 517 (1948–65)

Derby goals: 110

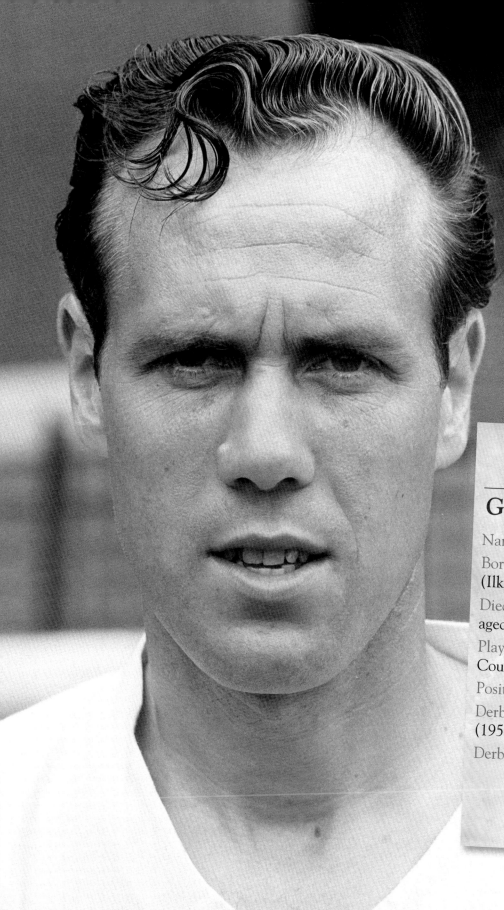

–LEGENDS–

Geoff Barrowcliffe

Like Parry, Barrowcliffe was a homegrown talent who went on to make more than 500 appearances for Derby, 475 of them in the league. Barrowcliffe began his career with Ilkeston Town before signing for the Rams and, by the time he left for Boston United 16 years later, he'd chalked up an impressive goalscoring record for a full-back, even if most of his goals did come from the penalty spot. After his professional days he remained a well-known figure on the local circuit and went on to play for Heanor Town and Long Eaton United, as well as Nottinghamshire sides Moor Green Colliery and Kimberley Town, after leaving the Baseball Ground.

FOOTBALL –STATS–

Geoff Barrowcliffe

Name: Geoffrey Barrowcliffe

Born: 18th October 1931 (Ilkeston)

Died: 26th September 2009; aged 77

Playing career: Derby County, Boston United

Position: Right-back

Derby appearances: 503 (1950–66)

Derby goals: 39

Derby remained in the Second Division for much of the Sixties but there were positives at the time, too, with the emergence of a couple of good, young players. Belper-born full-back Ron Webster was one of them. Webster was a senior and long-serving member of the squad by the time this picture was taken on 22nd January 1972. It shows the defender, and Rams keeper Colin Boulton, denying the Hammers' Clyde Best. Trevor Brooking, Frank Lampard and Bryan 'Pop' Robson scored for the home side, while Kevin Hector, Alan Hinton and Alan Durban were on target for the visitors in the 3-3 draw.

Welshman Alan Durban was another to make the breakthrough at the same time as Ron Webster, under new manager Tim Ward. The main image shows him swooping to score a headed goal against Southampton at the Baseball Ground on 10th September 1969. Durban's effort was sandwiched by strikes from Willie Carlin and Kevin Hector, with Derby winning 3-0. Inset, Durban is pictured at the pre-season photocall in 1965.

FOOTBALL
–STATS–

Kevin Hector

Name: Kevin James Hector

Born: 2nd November 1944 (Leeds)

Playing career: Bradford Park Avenue, Derby County, Vancouver Whitecaps, Boston United (loan), Burton Albion (loan), Derby County

Position: Inside-forward

Derby appearances: 589 (1966–78 and 1980–82)

Derby goals: 201

England appearances: 2

Hector is denied by Nottingham Forest keeper Alan Hill during a 2-0 defeat at the Baseball Ground on 29th November 1969.

> *He was like a Rolls-Royce to a normal car. He just seemed to have a bit extra, Kevin.*
>
> Ron Webster

–LEGENDS–

Kevin Hector

After more than a decade outside the top tier, Derby made a real statement of their intent to return there when manager Tim Ward snapped up Kevin Hector for £40,000. It was a considerable sum, even if Hector was already a proven goalscorer, but almost 600 appearances and 201 goals – second only to Steve Bloomer in the Rams' scoring charts – later, the man the fans affectionately dubbed "King" would have proved he was worth every penny and then some. Hector formed a fearsome partnership with John O'Hare, and his goals were vitally important not only in securing Derby's return to the First Division but twice helping them to the title.

"King" Kevin holds off Keith Coleman of West Ham on 27th October 1973 during a 0-0 draw, and lets fly against Arsenal at Highbury on 8th November 1975 (above), a game in which he scored the only goal.

Derby spent most of the Sixties in the old Second Division, meaning fans at the Baseball Ground rarely got to witness first hand the greats of the game. Cup matches, however, were different, and occasionally genius was on show in Derby. Manchester United star George Best is pictured here warranting the attentions of three home players. The game was an FA Cup third-round match played on Saturday, 22nd January 1966. Best struck twice that day, with Denis Law, twice, and David Herd also on target for United, who won 5-2. John Richardson, from the penalty spot, and Frank Upton, scored for Derby.

The Clough Years
1967-1973

1967 Brian Clough replaces Tim Ward and brings in Peter Taylor as his right-hand man; Derby reach the League Cup semi-finals but finish 18th in the league. **1968** Dave Mackay is signed from Tottenham, and the Rams take the Second Division title. **1969–70** Derby finish fourth in their first season back in the top flight, but are denied entry into European competition after a League disciplinary commission finds the club guilty of administration irregularities; Derby pay a transfer fee of £100,000-plus for the first time, to sign Terry Hennessey from Nottingham Forest. **1970** Derby win the Watney Cup. **1970–71** Colin Todd is snapped up for £170,000, and the club go on to finish ninth. **1971–72** The Rams don't lose a league game until mid-October, and that run lays the foundations for them to become champions of England for the first time. Derby beat Liverpool in their last game and are on holiday in Majorca when their triumph is confirmed. **1972–73** The European Cup brings star names such as Benfica and Eusébio to the Baseball Ground, but the adventure ends controversially against Juventus in the semi-finals. In October 1973, the Rams are then plunged into meltdown when Clough and Taylor resign following disputes with the board.

ABOVE: Clough takes time out from his managerial duties in 1969 to read and ~~~~r letters from his *Sunday Mirror* column.

BELOW: In his office at the Baseball Ground, on the morning of 30th October 1969. Derby had recorded a 3-0 home win against Crystal Palace in a League Cup tie the previous night, with two goals from Alan Hinton and one from Kevin Hector.

Nobody knew it at the time, of course, but the appointment of Brian Clough – made by Sam Longson, following a tip from Len Shackleton – and his assistant Peter Taylor in 1967 would forever change the course of Derby County's history. It was *the* golden age for the football club and a period which would play out like a soap opera. There were so many highs for everyone associated with the Rams, but those good times were often set against a backdrop of infighting between the management staff and board. Sometimes the arguments would be kept in-house, but on just as many occasions Derby's dirty laundry would be aired in public. That, though, added to the intrigue which surrounded the club at the time, and contributed almost as much to the interest being generated at the Baseball Ground as the success achieved on the field. Charismatic Clough, 32 at the start of his reign, and his trusty sidekick Taylor, actually finished one place lower in their first season in charge than Derby had managed in the previous campaign, but the foundations they laid that year and the summer that followed would see the club not only become a real force in English football but in Europe as well.

"*Brian was always sowing seeds. He'd come to me, as with other players, and say, 'I think you might need a haircut.' He'd remind you a couple of times one week and then it would go into the second week and he'd say, 'I think it's about time now that you did get your hair cut.' If you left it another week, you got the full repertoire when it was, 'If you don't get your hair cut, you'll be fined.' He always gave you a chance to get it cut and, if you didn't do it after that, you were in trouble big time.*"

Roy McFarland

Brian Clough in May 1969 with his children Elizabeth, 2, Nigel, 3, and Simon, 5. Thirty-nine-and-a-half years after this photograph was taken – and 36 years after Brian left the club – Nigel would follow in his father's footsteps by becoming Derby's manager.

The dream team

Clough and Taylor in the boardroom at the Baseball Ground in January 1973.

ABOVE: Derby's management team pictured at the Baseball Ground in August 1967 at the start of their first campaign in charge.

BELOW: A then 32-year-old Clough with Taylor and some of the Rams' first-team stars, taken in October 1967.

Taylor listens in as Clough hits the phone in his office at the stadium, also in October 1967.

Between them, Clough and Taylor forged one of the most famous partnerships in English football history, as they transformed Derby County from also-rans into a championship-winning team. Clough's man-management and Taylor's ability to spot a player where others couldn't, meant they complemented each other perfectly. However, it wasn't always the smoothest of relationships and, at times, it was downright hostile. So much so that, when Taylor died in 1990, the pair still weren't on speaking terms. But the legacy they left at Derby means that both, as individuals and as a double act, will forever be remembered with fondness and gratitude by everyone associated with the club.

KEN JONES talks about the trials of staying in top class

CLO

THE SILENCE t
Rangers these pas
Derby County and
into the First Divis

Rangers have not on
amongst the elite, but a

FIGHT AT THE TOP

	P.	W.	D.	L.	F.	A.	Pts
DERBY	38	22	11	5	54	31	55
C. PALACE	38	20	10	8	65	44	50
MIDDLESBRO'	39	19	10	10	55	43	48
CHARLTON	38	17	12	9	57	51	46

When the manager wins the bonus!

Lorraine Cabell, 17, was the players' choice as "Miss Derby County" . . . but manager Brian Clough seems to be raking in the bonus with a congratulatory kiss.

Lorraine (36-22-36), a hairdresser who thinks too few girls support County, "will

It's a tough job but somebody has to do it: Clough could be terrifying his players and staff one minute, as Roy McFarland attests, and then charming the hind legs off a donkey – or, in this case, Miss Derby County 1967 – the next. Either way, his magic began to work at Derby during that second season, when the club won promotion back to the First Division.

Jack Bowers was physio when I first joined Derby and Cloughie would make him tremble at times. I would worry about Jack. He'd be strapping my ankles because I'd get them done for every training session and I'd hear Brian coming down the corridor shouting, 'I hope there's no-one on those beds, Jack. I hope

GH: THIS IS ONLY THE START FOR US

...as settled on Queen's Park
...eeks should not be lost on
...e still bidding to follow them

...en relegated in their first season
...t forgotten in the process.

But even if a close study of Second Division form suggests there is no team who will do better, promotion is not without hope.

Jack Charlton, of Leeds and England, who is within reach of his first championship medal, recalls his club's arrival at the top and says: "If anything we found it easier than we did in the Second Division. We finished runners-up to Manchester United in our first season back and we would have won the championship if we had not faded towards the end.

"It's not easy to assess the chances of other teams because we went up with a lot of young players who had still to discover how good they really were.

"The very fact that they were prepared to run and fight stood us in good stead and few teams were prepared to match us.

"We were surprised at how well we did because our main aim was consolidation.

"I don't think we would do so well now because the First Division gets harder each season.

"But as long as the best of any team's young players can learn as they go along survival is far from impossible.

"I don't see much of Second Division football but when I do the difference between the divisions stands out.

"The standard of goal-keeping in the First Division is much higher.

"There are better wingers in the First Division. In fact in the Second you rarely see any.

"The standard of defensive play is higher. There is better organisation, defenders don't wander into bad positions and are not as guilty of following the ball and leaving a man unmarked.

Spirit

"People like Brian Clough and Dave Mackay at Derby will know all this and be prepared for it so they must have a chance.

"Teams who have come up and done well, ourselves, Liverpool, Manchester City, have kept the same players together as far as possible.

"I don't see any great value in scurrying around for new players. It only disrupts the spirit which has got the team up in the first place."

Derby manager Brian

THE LAST MATCHES

PALACE
Huddersfield
         (a, tomorrow)
Preston ... (a, Saturday)
Fulham ... (h, April 19)
Blackburn (a, April 28)

MIDDLESBROUGH
Norwich (h, tomorrow)
Bury ...... (h, Saturday)
Birmingham
         (a, April 19)

CHARLTON
Birmingham (a, today)
Huddersfield
         (a, Saturday)
Blackburn (h, April 15)
Preston ... (h, April 19)

Clough argues along the same line.

He said: "I believe we can do well in the First Division with the present staff of players. We like to think that this is only the beginning.

"However, I am hoping to sign at least two more men before next season to give us that extra bit of push.

"I am proud of the way the team has played, and I believe we have gone up because we are a talented side and not just a lot of workers."

Crystal Palace, Charlton and Middlesbrough must go on battling for the right to follow Derby up, and Palace now look clear favourites.

> *everyone's fit to start training.' Jack would be worried sick about it. I'd say, 'Don't worry, we're all right', and Brian would pop his head in. 'What are you bloody lot doing in here? Get out there. Jack, I don't want that lot in here having a cup of tea, get them out as soon as you can.' I'd have to say, 'Jack, some of us actually have knocks that need sorting out.'*
>
> Roy McFarland

Clough could be hard as nails when it came to dealing with his senior players, but he was always very protective of the young lads coming through the ranks at all of his clubs. This picture, with four young Derby hopefuls, was taken at the Baseball Ground in October 1967.

—LEGENDS—

Dave Mackay

Dave Mackay, at 34 and already a superstar, really broke the mould of Clough/Taylor signings when they took him to Derby in 1968, but his acquisition proved another masterstroke. The experience the Scotland international had gained at Tottenham – with whom he won the Double in 1960–61, the FA Cup two more times, in 1962 and 1967, and the UEFA Cup Winners' Cup in 1963 – was invaluable in what was an otherwise young team, and Derby reaped the rewards immediately. In his first season with the club, and despite playing in the Second Division, Mackay was recognized by his peers as the joint Professional Footballers' Association Footballer of the Year, along with Manchester City's Tony Book, as he helped the Rams to the title. Mackay would also captain the club to its first First Division crown in the 1971–72 season. When Clough left, Mackay was the man to whom Derby turned, and he was manager of the second championship-winning team. Not just a Derby legend, but an all-time great of the game.

I'M SORRY I LET DAVE GO —NICHOLSON

By NIGEL CLARKE

BILL NICHOLSON, manager of Spurs, said what Soccer fans have long suspected: "I'm sorry I sold Dave Mackay."

A match that began as a sentimental occasion for Mackay, Derby's old warrior, ended in the massacre of Tottenham.

Nicholson called the 5—0 defeat a "humiliation." His players were stunned into silence. But Mackay, with a melon-sized grin on his face, said: "This was a result beyond my wildest dreams."

Added Nicholson: "When I let Dave go, neither he nor I suspected his move would turn out like this. But good luck to him.

"I wish I had six Dave Mackays in my side, then I wouldn't have any worries."

When Nicholson let him go at the start of last season he said: "Dave no longer has the pace for the First Division."

He was right, but misjudged the tremendous influence that Mackay can have on a team.

He has helped mould Derby into a team that Nicholson calls "great."

Great Skill

The Spurs chief said: "Let nobody take anything away from Derby. They play it quick and simple. They have players who read the game well and have great skill, teamwork and the right blend. They are a fine side."

Said Mackay: "It was a great win for us, and a tremendous experience for me. It was also the best Derby have played since I've been with them.

"You don't expect to beat anybody by five goals in the First Division, and I was a little embarrassed at the end.

"It takes a big man to say we played well when his side has just been badly beaten. Bill Nicholson is just that."

"Still it's about time we had some praise. Until now everyone has called our unbeaten run just good luck."

Manager Brian Clough, who has built Derby into a side that can hold its head high in the First Division, was at the ground yesterday selling League Cup tickets for the game with Hull.

"I did it when we were bottom of the Second Division I'll do it now we are at the top of the First," he said.

"A little success won't change me. All I can say is that we are going to shock a lot more people before this season is through."

Diabolical

Spurs have now conceded ten goals in the last three games. Said Nicholson: "We were diabolical at the back. Have you ever seen Mike England play so badly?"

Spurs have injury worries. Roger Morgan has injured his ankle ligaments and he seen a specialist this morning about a toe he broke last season which has been giving him pain. John Pratt has damaged his back.

England was not the only Spurs player to struggle, and one player said yesterday: "Some of the things we did were diabolical. You cannot give a team like Derby a three-goal start."

> *I was blessed in terms of the players I played with and none more so than Dave Mackay. He feared nobody or anything in his life, and that rubbed off on to us. I was 19 when he signed, so the majority of us were young guys, young players developing our football, and this mega-star came into the football club who had done the Double with Tottenham, had played in Europe, captained Scotland, numerous international caps, and there he was playing at Derby County.*
>
> Roy McFarland

Dave Mackay in action against Arsenal in 1969 (main picture), and challenging Manchester City keeper Joe Corrigan the same year.

FOOTBALL
–STATS–
Dave Mackay

Name: David Craig Mackay

Born: 14th November 1934 (Edinburgh)

Playing career: Hearts, Tottenham, Derby County, Swindon

Position: Central defender

Managerial career: Swindon, Nottm Forest, Derby County, Walsall, Al-Arabi Kuwait, Al-Shabab, Al-Arabi Kuwait, Doncaster, Birmingham, Zamalek, Qatar

Derby appearances: 145 (1968–71)

Derby goals: 7

Scotland appearances: 22

Scotland goals: 4

Two magic moments..

THE moment of triumph for Dave Mackay. The final whistle has gone and the old Scots international raises his arms to salute Derby's victory over his old Tottenham colleagues. And Willie Carlin, after notching the third goal of their 5—0 win, runs up to give him a kiss of joy just to show how they feel about Dave in Derby.

Pictures: Monte Fresco

BELOW: Mackay and Tony Book receive their joint Player of the Year awards from Sir Alf Ramsey for the 1968–69 season. Mackay's old Tottenham boss, Bill Nicholson, later admitted he should never have let the Scot join Derby.

Second Division champions, 1968–69

Rams ace Kevin Hector leads the celebrations at a civic reception given for Derby's triumphant stars by the County Council at their Matlock HQ on 23rd April 1969, after the team were crowned Second Division champions. Assistant-manager Peter Taylor looks on, with Willie Carlin and Alan Durban taking in the jubilant scenes. Inset, the bus makes its way through Matlock towards the council offices. It had started its journey from Derby Mayor's Parlour and weaved its way through hoards of well-wishers lining the streets of Duffield, Belper, Wirksworth, Cromford and Matlock Bath before reaching its destination.

Multiple celebrations followed the Second Division title victory, including a parade through the streets of Derby.

First Division Derby … again

Derby County's pre-season photocall at the Baseball Ground in July 1969. Back row, left to right: Frank Wignall, Alan Durban, Les Green, Ron Webster, John Robson, Roy McFarland and Jim Walker. Front row, left to right: John McGovern, Willie Carlin, Dave Mackay, Kevin Hector, John O'Hare and Alan Hinton.

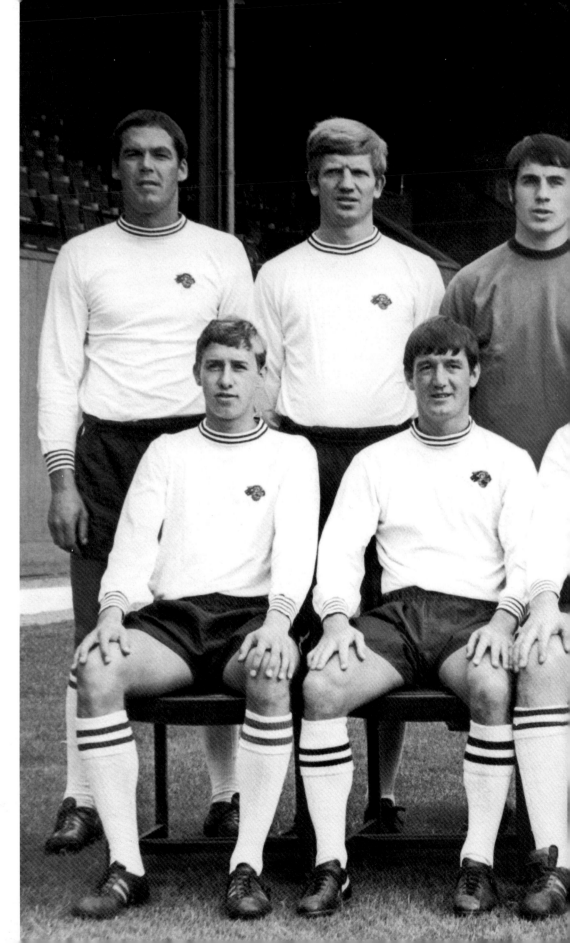

71

Mirror SPORTLIGHT

From RON WILLS Derby, Thursday

DERBY'S £200,000 stand is ready . . . the players are fit and rarin' to go . . . the fans are optimistic. But the men who run the show are in grim mood.

First Division football is back in this Midland town after sixteen years But if it's entertainment you're after—forget it.

Assistant manager Peter Taylor says: "We're here to do a job. To win."

And manager Brian Clough adds: "The fans want success. As long as their team isn't losing, they're happy. Two seasons ago we scored eight-seven goals but finished fifth from the bottom of the table. Nooody cared.

"Last season we won the Second Division championship with only sixty-five goals—and the town went wild. So don't talk to me about entertainment.

"More managers have been sacked trying to play attacking football, than I've had hot dinners. It's just not on these days."

Clough, manager of Derby for just twenty-six months, has a first team pool of only thirteen players.

He says: "The money is available to buy new talent, but players just aren't available. We'll sweat it out for two months and see how our present staff shapes up."

CLOUGH is about to sign a new five-year contract which will make him one of the highest paid managers in Soccer. And the players are a long way off the breadline, too. They get a bonus every week they keep out of the bottom eight places. Says Clough: "I got the players good money because it would be ridiculous if they felt financially inferior to the teams they meet."

BRIAN CLOUGH
. new contract

CHAIRMAN Sydney Bradley authorised the new wage structure—and the £200,000 stand. He says: "We feel it is right to cash in on success. Now we have a team every bit as good as the one we had in the forties, with Raich Carter and Peter Doherty."

ADVANCE season ticket sales have already paid for the new stand. And there are bumper gates ahead. Chairman Bradley said: "Manchester United and Spurs are the two teams most people want to see at the Baseball Ground. And what a marvellous moment for Dave Mackay when Spurs do come."

QUOTE . . . from Clough on life as a manager: "It's a jungle. Sometimes the lack of honesty in the sport disturbs me. It is, after all, only a job. A well-paid one—but just a job. And I think if the game and its intrigues ever got me down or interfered with my private life I'd get out of it altogether. Sometimes I think it is only the fact that I know nothing but football that has prevented me from getting out before."

SKIPPER Mackay is now 35, but reckons he still has another couple of seasons left with Derby. The highlight of the season for him will be leading Derby out to play Spurs at White Hart Lane. He says: "Playing at the back doesn't demand so much of me. And I still think I have something to offer the team."

LAST LINE . . . Clough, asked what he hoped to achieve during the period of his new five-year contract, replied: "I expect Derby to win something—and I don't mean the Second Division championship again."

Derby's return to the top flight in 1969 heralded another new chapter and, as the *Mirror* recorded on 8th August that year, chairman Sydney Bradley helped move things forward again that summer when he oversaw the addition of a new £200,000 stand and authorized a new wage structure, which befitted a First Division club. Clough, too, was to be rewarded with a new five-year deal and everything looked rosy, with Bradley claiming the team was every bit as good as the one of Carter and Doherty, which won the FA Cup in the Forties. The positivity which surrounded the club at the time, however, did not last long, and just three months later cracks began to appear in the relationship between manager and board. Clough had been offered his new contract at the start of the season but it remained unsigned and, when news broke that Catalan giants Barcelona were keen to take him to the Nou Camp, Bradley questioned whether the interest in his manager was genuine or self-generated. Unsurprisingly, Clough hit the roof and announced he was willing to listen to offers not just from Barça but from any club.

> "
> *The signing of Willie Carlin in the early part of 1968 gave us grit and determination. He was a good footballer and had a good football brain, and he was the one who made us gel together, made us click. That was a magnificent signing. We never looked back from there.*
> "
>
> Roy McFarland

ABOVE: Willie Carlin wheels away in delight after scoring in a 3-0 win against Southampton at the Baseball Ground on 10th September 1969. Goals from Alan Durban and Kevin Hector sandwiched Carlin's effort.

LEFT: Derby were far from overshadowed by their rivals during that first season back in the First Division, and went on to finish the campaign in fourth place. Here Manchester United goalkeeper Alex Stepney beats John O'Hare to a cross.

73

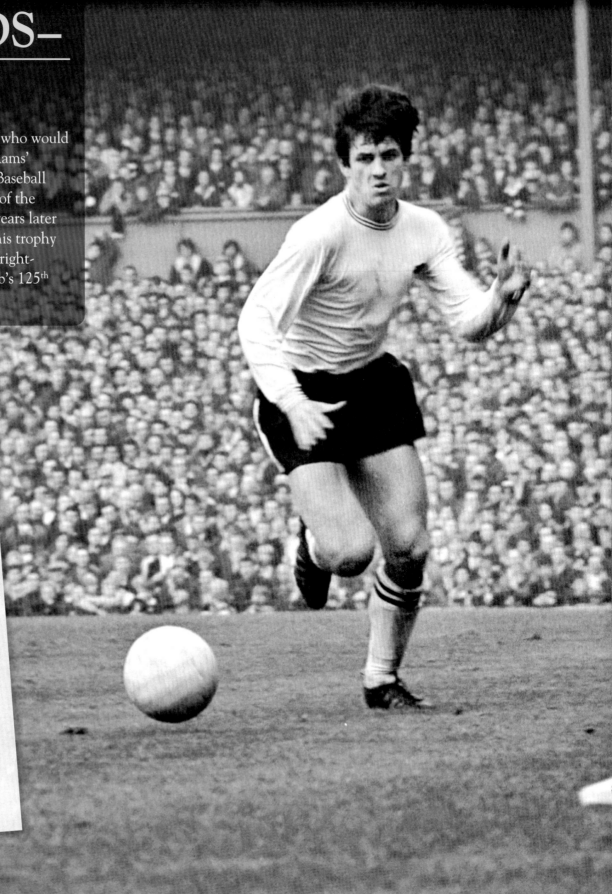

–LEGENDS–

Ron Webster

Ron Webster was another local lad who would go on to become a member of the Rams' 500 Club in an 18-year stay at the Baseball Ground. Webster was voted Player of the Year in 1973–74 and retired three years later with two championship medals in his trophy cabinet. He was voted Derby's best right-back in a 2009 poll to mark the club's 125th anniversary celebrations.

FOOTBALL –STATS–

Ron Webster

Name: Ron Webster

Born: 21st June 1943 (Belper)

Playing career: Derby County, Minnesota Kicks

Position: Right-back

Derby appearances: 535 (1960–78)

Derby goals: 7

Left-back John Robson only missed one game all season as the Rams were crowned champions for the first time, but was still sold to Aston Villa at the end of the campaign. He went on to win the League Cup twice with Villa before he was forced to retire in 1978, at the age of 28, because he was suffering from multiple sclerosis. Robson died in 2004, aged 53, after a long battle with the disease.

He's here, he's there …

Derby had a fine first season back in the First Division, with John O'Hare's goals and his partnership with Kevin Hector a major factor in their success. Here, in front of a full house at the Baseball Ground on 29th November 1969, the Scottish international tries to beat Nottingham Forest's Peter Hindley to the ball. Sadly, the visitors won the game 2-0 thanks to goals from Ian Storey-Moore and Barry Lyons. But the Rams had the last laugh: they finished fourth that season, 11 places above their arch-enemy. One of the most popular chants at the Baseball Ground during the late Sixties and Seventies was about the Scot, with Rams fans regularly bellowing, 'He's here, he's there, he's every-f******-where John O'Hare …' According to legend, O'Hare once asked supporters to tone it down a little bit. 'He's here, he's there, he's asked us not to swear …,' they sang in response.

Despite finishing fourth in the First Division in the 1969–70 season, Derby were denied entry into European competition in the following campaign and fined £10,000 after a League commission found the club guilty of administration irregularities. Rams officials met with the FA, who were probing the club's financial affairs, at the Cavendish Hotel in London's Lancaster Gate on 3rd April 1970. Derby were represented, left to right, by Sir Robertson King (president), Alan Collard (club secretary), Sydney Bradley (chairman), Mr Mason (club auditor) and Ken Turner.

79

The Rams are put through their paces at Colwick Woods in Nottingham on 13th July 1970 as part of a gruelling pre-season training camp. Leading the running drill (front right, bottom left picture) is former Forest defender Terry Hennessey, who had joined Derby in a £100,000-plus transfer from the City Ground five months earlier.

The Watney Cup

Roy McFarland rattles home Derby's first goal after Dave Mackay's free-kick had hit a post. Alan Hinton scored the second, Alan Durban the third and Mackay the fourth, while George Best scored for United.

A short-lived competition in the early Seventies, the Watney Cup – so called because it was sponsored by the Watney Mann brewery – was a pre-season tournament contested by the teams who had scored the most goals in their respective divisions during the previous campaign but had not been promoted or admitted to European competition. Two teams from each of the four divisions took part, with Derby and Manchester United from the First Division, Hull and Sheffield United from the Second Division, Fulham and Reading from the Third Division, and Aldershot and Peterborough from the Fourth Division contesting the 1970 tournament. Derby beat Fulham in the quarter-finals and Sheffield United in the semi-finals, while Manchester United beat Hull in the last four to set up a clash at the Baseball Ground, which Derby won 4-1.

Mackay's men master hesitant Sheffield United

McGOVERN DRIVE PUTS DERBY INTO FINAL

By PETER INGALL
Derby 1, Sheff Utd 0

DERBY surged into the Watney Cup final last night with one of the best goals scored on the Baseball Ground for some time.

They had fought hard for thirty minutes to break down the tough and well-packed Sheffield defence when right winger John McGovern's shot put them through to a home tie in the final on Saturday.

Left winger Alan Hinton hit the right-wing corner into a crowded goalmouth and the ball was headed out by Sheffield defender John Flynn.

The ball went to McGovern, 20, who is fighting to establish a regular place in the first team.

He brilliantly controlled the ball with his back to goal and then turned to go round Colin Addison. He suddenly saw a gap and hit a 20-yard shot into the corner of the net.

It was a tremendous effort which brought the crowd to their feet, and which deserved to win a match Derby had dominated for most of the 90 minutes.

The only time Derby looked to be in trouble was seven minutes before they scored.

Scare

A through ball found United's Welsh international Gil Reece deep in the Derby half. He neatly beat full back Ron Webster before speeding goalwards only to be brought down on the edge of the penalty area by Derby's skipper Dave Mackay.

Apart from this scare, Derby were never in real trouble, and only some lucky deflection and hesitancy in front of goal stopped them from winning by a bigger margin.

Roy McFarland had a shot deflected wide, Flynn kicked off the line from Kevin Hector, and Hector saw another good effort pushed round the post by goalkeeper Alan Hodgkinson.

Late in the second half Alan Durban put in a header which bounced off the United goalkeeper's chest.

In defence Mackay was again the driving force. He received good support from left back John Robson and McFarland. The Sheffield forwards lacked bite and failed miserably to cash in on some smart midfield work.

WATNEY'S CUP
Semi-Finals

Derby .... 1 Sheff Utd 0
McGovern   H-T 1—0 9
                                25,321

Hull .... 1 Man Utd 1
Chilton   Law
(a.e.t.) H.T. 1—0   54,007
(after extra time, Man. Utd. won on penalty kicks)

Sheffield United's Eddie Colquhoun leaps high to head clear a Derby attack.

Dave Mackay lifts the trophy for Derby while Bobby Charlton looks on as the jubilant Rams celebrate.

A midfield Gem

Archie Gemmill is all smiles on 22nd September 1970 as he leaves Preston North End after signing for Derby.

Clough had to be at his persuasive best to convince Archie Gemmill to sign for Derby, and even invited himself to stay overnight at the Scot's home after being told the player was still unsure whether or not he wanted to move to the Baseball Ground. The following morning Gemmill's wife, Betty, cooked the pair a hearty breakfast over which Clough finalized negotiations and got his man to sign. Midfielder Gemmill spent seven years at the Baseball Ground and was captain in Roy McFarland's absence for much of the 1974–75 season, at the end of which Derby won the First Division for the second time. Gemmill left Derby in 1977, following Clough down the road to Nottingham Forest.

> *[Archie] was up and down that field like a horse.*
>
> Alan Hinton

Mirror Sport

Tuesday, October 30, 1973
Telephone: (STD code 01)—353 0246

12-1 DOUBLE

Bouverie landed a 12-1 double at Nottingham yesterday. His nap Dolphinetto won at 3-1 and his next best Great Freda came in at 9-4. Great Freda was napped by Tim Richards and was also the Topspot.

JOIN THE WINNING *Racing Mirror*
Pages 24 and 25

Getting ahead in style..
Page 23

STARS SWAP BID IS TURNED DOWN
Page 26

LIVERPOOL WIN BIG CUP CLASH
Page 27

DERBY ESCAPE

Gemmill grabs another replay

DERBY must face Second Division Sunderland yet again to decide who goes into the third round of the League Cup.

Derby survived through an 80th minute goal by Archie Gemmill at Roker last night, but extra-time left the teams still locked at 1–1.

It was Sunderland the battling Cup fighters who never know when they are beaten who made the first major impact.

Winger Dennis Tueart gave the game the spark it needed when he chased a poor back-pass by Roy McFarland in the twenty-first minute and was brought down by Derby keeper Colin Boulton.

Referee Ray Tinkler had no hesitation in pointing to the penalty spot.

Tueart took the kick himself — and Boulton made amends by flinging himself to his right and blocking the shot with his body.

Desperate

Sunderland full back Joe Bolton followed up with a volley that Archie Gemmill desperately hooked away from the line and the tie was well and truly alive.

Seven minutes later Vic Halom put the ball in the Derby net but with the assistance of his hand.

Then, in the 21st minute, fighting Sunderland got the goal they had been hunting for.

Dave Watson, rising high to a corner, forced Boulton to punch away—but only to Tueart, whose shot was in the net

before the defence could blink.

It was clearly a relief to Tueart after his earlier lapse.

Then the hard-worked Boulton had to go full stretch to put out an effort by Billy Hughes.

Derby had been properly thrown out of joint in a game that was fast building up to a classic.

Roger Davies was booked three minutes before half-time for a foul on Watson.

The thrills continued to come thick and fast after the break as Derby pressed hard for the equaliser.

In a last throw of the dice, manager Dave Mackay sent on former Roker favourite John O'Hare as a replacement for John McGovern thirteen minutes from time.

Three minutes later, a moment of indecision by Sunderland's defence let in Gemmill for a goal that sent the match into extra time.

By COLIN DIBALL
Sunderland . . . 1
Derby 1
(after extra time.)

RESULTS

LEAGUE CUP
Second Rnd Replays

Escape! Derby's Archie Gemmill clears the Sunderland shot that followed a penalty save by 'keeper Colin Boulton.

Gemmill makes headlines in the *Mirror* on Tuesday, 30th October 1973, after scoring the goal which earned Derby a 1-1 draw at Sunderland's old Roker Park stadium the previous night. A day later, Sunderland won the second replay, again at Roker Park, 3-0.

In action during a 2-2 draw with Arsenal in the fifth round of the FA Cup on 26th February 1972. Alan Durban and Alan Hinton bagged the goals for Derby.

LEGENDS

Colin Todd

One of the most elegant defenders to have graced the game, Todd signed from Sunderland for £170,000 and became a rock at the heart of Derby's defence alongside Roy McFarland and, when he was injured, Peter Daniel. Todd played 293 league matches for Derby, won the club's Player of the Year award during the first championship-winning campaign and, in the 1974–75 season, when the Rams won their second crown, was honoured with the highest individual accolade in English football when he was voted Player of the Year by the Professional Footballers Association.

Colin Todd holds off Trevor Brooking during a goalless draw at Upton Park on 27th October 1973.

FOOTBALL –STATS–

Colin Todd

Name: Colin Todd

Born: 12th December 1948 (Chester-le-Street)

Playing career: Sunderland, Derby County, Everton, Birmingham City, Nottm Forest, Oxford, Vancouver Whitecaps, Luton

Position: Central defender

Managerial career: Middlesbrough, Bolton, Swindon, Derby County, Bradford City, Randers FC, Darlington, Randers FC

Derby appearances: 371 (1971–78)

Derby goals: 10

England appearances: 27

Todd signing for Derby on 19th February 1971 under the watchful eyes of Brian Clough and Peter Taylor.

Something special is happening ...

Derby made a blistering start to the league campaign and went into October unbeaten as they built on the impressive fourth-place finish of the previous season. Brian Clough's side were in and around the leading pack throughout and, as the season reached its climax, they were still in with a shout. Liverpool and Leeds were also in the hunt in a nail-biting finale, with the Merseysiders providing Derby's opposition at the Baseball Ground for the Rams' final game of the season.

LEFT: Alan Hinton is watched by a full house at Stamford Bridge as Derby visit Chelsea on 18th September 1971. The game ended 1-1, with Roy McFarland on target for the Rams.

RIGHT: John O'Hare in full flow against Arsenal on 12th February 1972, a game Derby lost 2-0.

We've done all we can ...

John McGovern fires the ball past Liverpool defender Tommy Smith, with John O'Hare looking on, to score the only goal of the game and defeat the Rams' title rivals at the Baseball Ground on 1st May 1972. The victory meant Derby, having completed their season, were top of the table with second-placed Leeds a point behind. But Leeds still had one game still to play ...

Just champions

The *Mirror* back page on Tuesday, 9th May, confirmed what Derby's players – who by then were on holiday in Majorca – and the rest of the country had learned the night before: that the Rams' title rivals Leeds had lost 2-1 to Wolves, meaning Clough's men, for the first time in the club's history, were champions of England. It was an incredible achievement and one which sparked scenes of hysteria throughout the county. Derby's players, as the report revealed, listened to the last few moments of the Leeds game on the radio and the celebrations on the Balearic isle went on well into the night. No wonder there were a few bleary eyes the next day …

Oh, this year we're off to sunny Spain …

Alan Durban, standing, takes no chances in the Majorca sunshine, reapplying the suntan lotion while Colin Boulton, lying down, soaks up the rays.

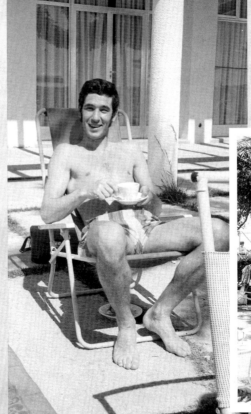

ABOVE: John Robson celebrates the title triumph with the drink of champions … a lovely cup of tea.

BELOW: Likely lads Alan Hinton, Alan Durban and Terry Hennessey enjoy their time in the sun.

93

Sombrero superstars, from left to right: Terry Hennessey, John O'Hare, Alan Durban, Colin Boulton, Alan Hinton, John McGovern, Ron Webster and John Robson.

Assistant-manager Peter Taylor and striker Roger
Davies pose with the First Division trophy in the
boardroom at the Baseball Ground in January 1973.
Hitman Davies played 166 times for Derby in two
spells, from 1971–76 and 1979–80, scoring 44 goals.

LEGENDS

Roy McFarland

Roy McFarland was just 19 when Brian Clough and Peter Taylor took him to Derby, and he soon established himself as one of the finest centre-halves in England. He was at the heart of Derby's defence, alongside Dave Mackay, as the club won the Second Division and then the First Division, and later forged an equally impressive partnership with Colin Todd. McFarland made 500-plus appearances in two spells for Derby, and later played a significant role in the management set-up, acting as caretaker-manager in the Eighties after Peter Taylor was sacked, and as assistant to Arthur Cox in the Nineties, before taking over following Cox's departure.

FOOTBALL -STATS-

Roy McFarland

Name: Roy Leslie McFarland

Born: 5th April 1948 (Liverpool)

Playing career: Tranmere, Derby County, Bradford City, Derby County

Position: Central defender

Managerial career: Bradford City, Derby County, Bolton (co-manager), Cambridge United, Torquay, Chesterfield, Burton Albion

Derby appearances: 530 (1967–81 and 1983–84)

Derby goals: 48

England appearances: 28

Roy McFarland rests up in his garden as he recovers from an Achilles injury in 1974. He tussles with Tottenham's Alan Gilzean during a 1-0 league defeat at White Hart Lane on 29th September 1973, and in action against West Ham in February 1971. The Rams won that game at Upton Park 4-1, with two goals apiece from Kevin Hector and Alan Hinton.

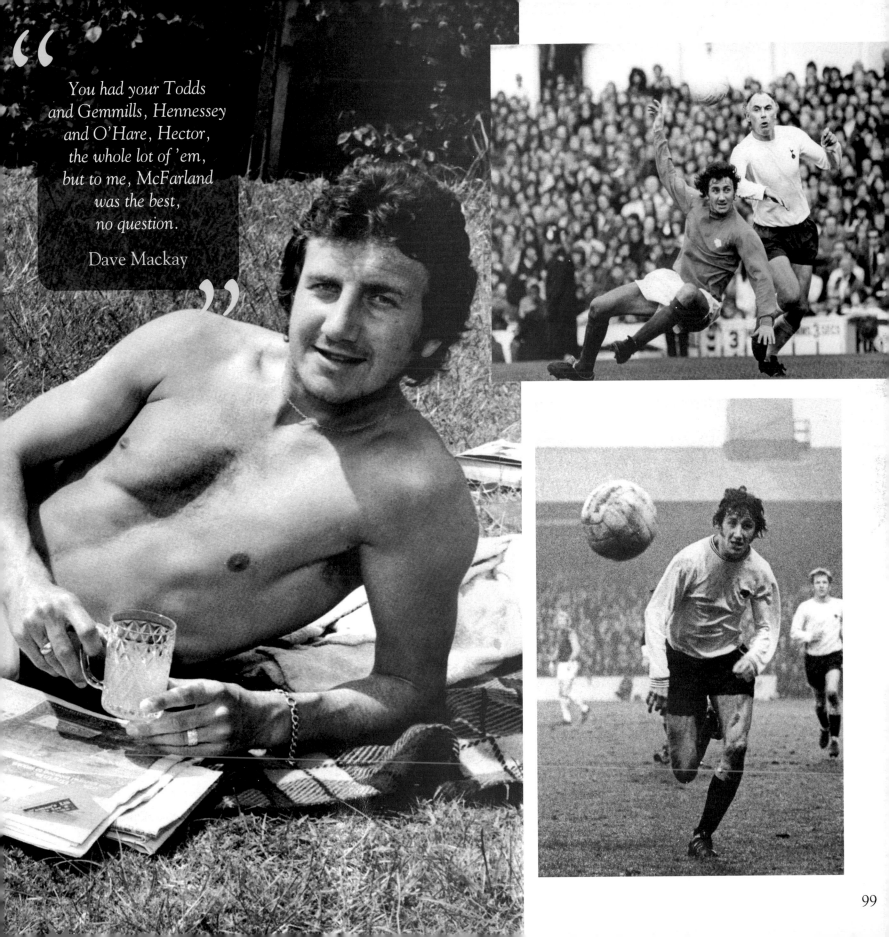

> "You had your Todds and Gemmills, Hennessey and O'Hare, Hector, the whole lot of 'em, but to me, McFarland was the best, no question."
>
> Dave Mackay

Benfica legend Eusébio (second left) looks helplessly on as Roy McFarland gives Derby the lead in their European Cup second-round, first-leg clash on 25th October 1972, and, right, our pictures show the celebration which followed. The Rams completely outplayed the Portuguese giants, winning 3-0, with further goals from Kevin Hector and John McGovern. A fortnight later, Derby travelled to Benfica's famous Estádio Da Luz (Stadium of Light), and a magnificent display from goalkeeper Colin Boulton saw the Rams hold their hosts to a 0-0 draw to claim the aggregate victory.

Mirror Sport

Thursday, October 26, 1972
Telephone: (STD code 01)—353 0246

EUROPE CRUNCH NIGHT

Spurs in four-goal Cup romp
Page 31

Wrexham shatter Yugoslavs
Pages 30, 31

Derby's Kevin Hector just fails to score.

GREAT DERBY!

Treble blast hits Benfica

Derby 3, Benfica 0

DERBY COUNTY once again reserved their most impressive form for their European Cup challenge.

The Eagles of Benfica will have to fly very high indeed if they are to get over the mountainous task created them by Derby last night.

The only regret about Derby's performance is that they did not manage to maintain the pressure which produced three first half goals and could have provided many more.

Effective

But maybe that is carping. There must still be admiration for them all, and for four in particular—Colin Todd and Ray McFarland in defence and John O'Hare and Kevin Hector in attack.

From the start, reputations meant nothing to Derby.

From the start their weapons were the simple, effective ones—pace, urgency, power.

Benfica, used to a more leisurely pace, must have felt at times that they were at war against the Chinese army, as the Derby hordes kept pouring forward at them.

Inside the first minute goalkeeper Jose Henriques had to go down desperately at Kevin Hector's feet to save—and for the rest of the half had to do more work than he has done all season.

His defenders must take their share of the blame for the three goals which went past him in that first forty-five minutes.

In the eighth minute, when Gemmill touched a short corner to Alan Hinton, no one moved to meet the menace of Roy McFarland, racing unmarked, once again, lenged to meet the cross and head it home with authority.

That was just the start of it, pounding for Henriques. He punched away a Hinton drive as O'Hare flattened him. He got down brilliantly low to his right to turn a

It's there . . . Derby salute Roy McFarland's opening goal.

By FRANK McGHEE

drive from Hector away. But he was let down, and left stranded, once again in the twenty-seventh minute—although he can't escape all the blame.

This time — when Hinton took a corner—McFarland's challenge was blocked — but the ball broke out to Hector on the corner of the penalty area.

As he hooked it almost casually back, no Benfica man moved—including Henriques—as it floated just inside the post.

And how Hector missed the easiest chance of the night five minutes later—a header from five yards—neither he nor I, nor Henriques, will ever know.

Benfica were beginning to look distinctly tattered by the fortieth minute when their central defender, Messias, missed an interception and let John McGovern in for the left-foot shot which made it 3—0.

Danger

In all this time, Benfica had done remarkably little. The great Eusebio seemed more concerned with directing operations than taking part in them.

The only moment of much danger for Derby came when John Robson blocked a shot that centre-forward Batista had only half-hit

with Boulton moving the wrong way.

Benfica simply did not know what was hitting them most of the time. The distance and difference between their fabulous modern Stadium of Light to Derby's homespun Baseball Ground, cannot be measured merely in miles.

But Derby proved that the gap can be bridged by football.

Benfica brought on their 19-year-old wonder boy, Jordao, in place of Eusebio—in place of Baptista in the fifty-fourth minute. But he didn't do much better than the old one!

Eusebio did, however, get within inches of a goal with worrying frequency as Derby started to slacken off.

In the sixty-ninth minute he turned to flick at a corner and whipped it just wide of the far post.

And five minutes from time Eusebio ruffled Derby's composure with a darting raid which finished with a shot into the side netting.

VANISHING TRAWLER ALMOST HOME

Danish trawler Nordkap which sailed from Aberdeen harbour on Sunday with only cook aboard, sighted ten miles off Danish coast late last night.

Dalglish pops up to save Celtic blushes

By CHRIS HARRIGAN

CELTIC, Britain's first winners of the European Cup, faced a disastrous result last night.

They were drawing 1-1 before a 55,000 Glasgow crowd against Hungarians Ujpest Dozsa—the team Celtic k'o'd last season.

But then Kenny Dalglish, who had earlier scored an equaliser, hit the winner in the eightieth minute.

Hibernian gave the Scots something to cheer, however, by beating F C Besa of Albania 7-1 in the Cup Winners' Cup first-leg clash.

One of the night's biggest shocks happened in Rumania. Real Madrid, six times winners of the European Cup, plunged to a 2-1 defeat from unknown Pitesti Arges.

STOKE WANT GARY FOR ONE MATCH

By JACK STEGGLES

STOKE manager Tony Waddington hopes to borrow Gary Sprake from Leeds to play in goal in Saturday's home game against Leicester.

Then Waddington, left with a goalkeeping problem following Gordon Banks's car accident, will push through a £100,000 deal for Aberdeen's Scottish international keeper Bobby Clark.

Waddington decided to ask for Sprake, who has been displaced by David Harvey as Leeds' No. 1 goalkeeper, despite signing £35,000 Mike McDonald from Clydebank on Tuesday.

Stoke plan to complete the transfer of Clark after Saturday's match. Waddington re-opened negotiations with Aberdeen yesterday and Clark will meet Stoke officials today before returning home to play against Celtic on Saturday.

WIGNALL SENT OFF

Frank Wignall, Mansfield's former England centre forward, was sent off for dissent just before half-time at Hereford last night. He had been booked a minute earlier. Mansfield were beaten 3-1.

Printed and Published by DAILY MIRROR NEWSPAPERS, Ltd. (01-353 0246) at, and for t P C Newspapers, Ltd., Holborn Circus, London EC1P 1DQ. Registered at the Post Office as a newspaper.   © Daily Mirror Newspapers, Ltd., 1972

L7

Perhaps unsurprisingly, the following day's *Mirror* led with that amazing victory over one of the giants of European football. Little Derby, the team from the East Midlands who had yo-yoed between the divisions over the past 84 years, were suddenly carrying British hopes on their shoulders, and stars of the world game were not only coming to play at the Baseball Ground but were packed off defeated as well. "From the start, reputations meant nothing to Derby," wrote Frank McGhee of the game. "From the start their weapons were the simple, effective ones – pace, urgency, power." It was a fantastic result and a night that lives on in the memory of those fortunate enough to be there. But still there was work to be done …

Derby's victory over the Portuguese giants earned them a quarter-final tie against Slovakian side Spartak Trnava. Derby lost the first leg in Trnava – then part of Czechoslovakia – 1-0, but won the second leg 2-0 to claim an aggregate victory. Here Kevin Hector slams home the vital goal at the Baseball Ground to put Derby into the semi-finals.

… not that anyone should have doubted Clough's men. There were some big players in that side and one of them was always ready to step up when needed. Goalkeeper Colin Boulton was the man who did so in the Stadium of Light, his first-half heroics ensuring Benfica weren't able to get the quick, early goal they so desperately required. Boulton, quite rightly, took the plaudits in the *Mirror* the following day.

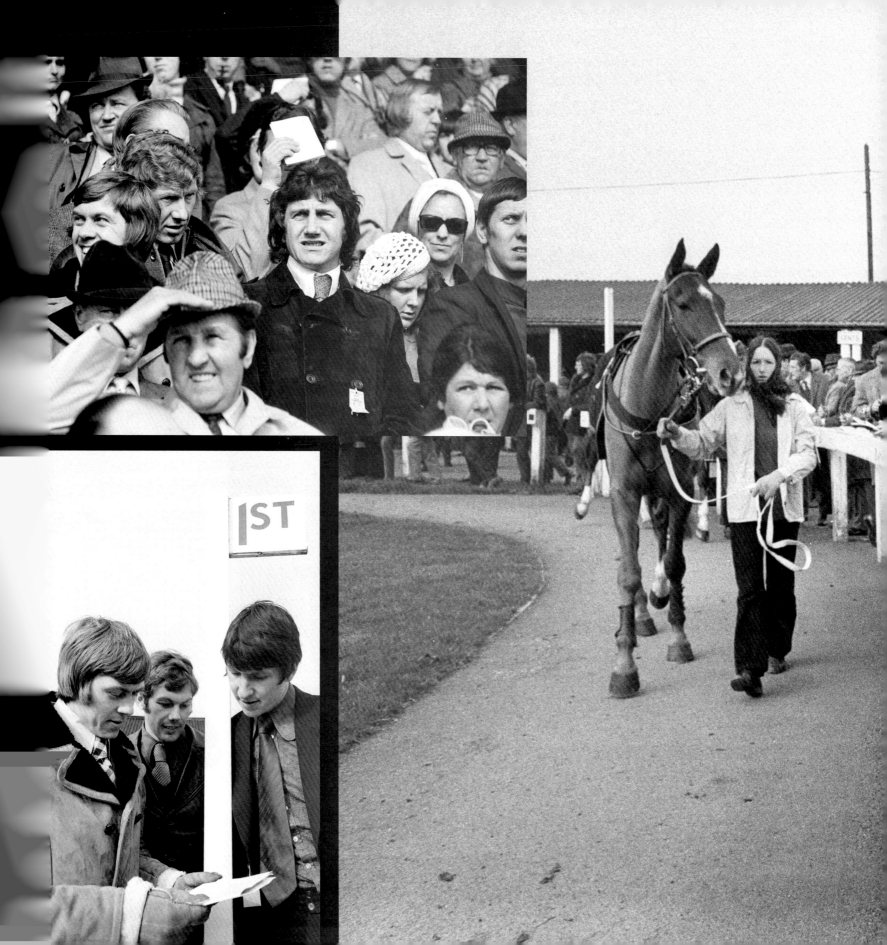

Brian Clough always put great emphasis on team spirit and, in March 1973, in the midst of their European battles, he packed his players off to Uttoxeter Races for the day to get their minds off football. Roger Davies, David Nish and Peter Daniel check out the runners and riders and their form (main picture and inset bottom left), while Roy McFarland and Alan Hinton (inset top left) enjoy a grandstand view.

Juventus and Italy legend Dino Zoff saves at the feet of Rams striker Kevin Hector, with midfielder Fabio Capello, who would go on to manage England from 2008 to 2012, loitering in the background. Meanwhile Brian Clough, Peter Taylor and the Derby bench, inset, don't look overly happy with events unfolding on the pitch.

The first leg of Derby's European Cup semi-final clash with
Juventus in Turin remains the most controversial game in
Rams history. Suspicions that something was amiss during
the first half – key men Roy McFarland and Archie Gemmill,
already on bookings, were shown yellow cards, which would
rule them out of the return leg for innocuous challenges – were
compounded at the interval when Peter Taylor went to talk
to West German referee Gerhard Schulenburg. He found the
official talking to his compatriot, Helmut Haller, the Juventus
forward, and was furious as he stormed back to Derby's own
changing room. There were suggestions that Derby should not
go back out for the second half. They did return to the field
but went on to lose the game 3-1. Kevin Hector scored Derby's
only goal, cancelling out José Altafini's effort in the first half,
before further goals from Francesco Causlo and another from
Altafini settled the first leg. Following that game Clough, in
his usual succinct manner, told Italian reporters who were
congregated outside Derby's changing room and desperate for a
quote: "No cheating b******s will I talk to, I'll not talk to any
cheating b******s!"

EUROPEAN CUP SHOCK

DISASTER DAY FOR DERBY— TWO MISS RETURN

DERBY boss Brian Clough screams at his men . . . Archie Gemmill gets booked . . . and only goalscorer Kevin Hector (below) has reason to be happy.

FRANK McGHEE

REPORTING
FROM TURIN
WEDNESDAY

Juventus 3, Derby Co 1

DERBY COUNTY flew home from Italy tonight still stubbornly insisting that they are not out of the European Cup—yet.

But, if they are honest, they ought not to dispute that they should be.

They could have finished the first leg of this semi-final trailing so far behind Juventus that snowballs in hell would be rated better insurance risks.

As well as the three goals they scored, Juventus also hit a post—and had two shots blocked on the line with keeper Colin Boulton beaten.

Gloomy

To add to Derby's problems, two of their most experienced internationals, centre half Roy McFarland and midfield man Archie Gemmill, will not be eligible for the second leg at home in a fortnight — because both were booked for the second time in the competition.

It all looks very gloomy — yet the irony of it is that for a full hour Derby were comfortably, calmly, in control.

The first twenty minutes in fact threatened to make this the non-event of a sporting lifetime — stifled by the Italian team's exaggerated caution.

Juventus gave Derby's two strikers, Kevin Hector and John O'Hare, a personal sentry each and kept sweeper Salvadore lurking handily in case either wriggled free.

Their own two most dangerous strikers, Anastasi and Altafini, were just as severely restricted at the other end.

It would have been more like a non-aggression pact than a football match in midfield at this stage but for the presence of a busy little fury of a fellow called Francesco Furini.

He dashed about doing most of his niggling damage after the ball had gone—and was the provocative cause of Gemmill's booking in the twenty-fourth minute.

By then Derby seemed to have been lulled into a dangerous belief that the strolling pace and absence of menace would last the ninety minutes.

More and more of their men came pushing forward, including at one stage both full backs, Ron Webster and David Nish.

Drifting

More and more defensive avenues were being opened for the sort of exploitation that is an Italian Soccer speciality—the sort that brought their opening goal in the twenty-eighth minute.

Anastasi, drifting out to the wing in search of a less crowded hunting ground, suddenly pounced to rob Webster, and crossed for Altafini to score with a fine right-foot drive.

If that goal was typically Italian, Derby's equaliser within a minute was typically British. It began with O'Hare chasing a ball the Italian defenders didn't believe he could possibly get.

The spirit that kept O'Hare going throughout a tremendous buffeting proved them wrong and, from his pass, Hector went on to score.

The game was back at square one, though just before half-time Derby had a distinctly ragged spell in which McFarland was booked for a foul on Cuccureddu and Nish kicked a shot from Marchetti off the line.

With composure restored, however, the second half was resuming a tranquil pattern.

Tracing back what went wrong, why it all changed, leads directly to the substitution Juventus made in the sixty-second minute, when the veteran German mercenary, Helmut Haller, came on for Cuccureddu in midfield.

He immediately starting prompting, encouraging and inspiring the men around him.

He made the significant pass in the six-man move which led to Juventus's second goal by Causio three minutes later—and that was the abrupt end of Derby supremacy.

In the eighty-second minute, Altafini, the Brazilian who at 34 is like a great wine — getting better and smoother and richer with age—crowned his own personal performance with a marvellous run to collect an Anastasi pass and a perfectly placed scoring shot.

Pictures
MONTE FRESCO

Cruyff and Co face KO

AJAX 2, Real Madrid 1

AJAX, fighting for a successive European Cup triumph, face exit after Real Madrid, six times winners of the trophy, restricted them to a one-goal lead in Amsterdam.

Second half goals by Barry Hulshoff and Rudi Krol seemed to have put Ajax—whose Johann Cruyff was tightly controlled—in command, but Pirri replied late

Leeds and England, Allan Clarke is escorted off by trainer Les Cocker at Elland Road last night.

GOAL ACE CLARKE SENT OFF

By DEREK WALLIS: Leeds 1, Hajduk Split 0

ALLAN CLARKE was sent off in an explosive incident in this first leg of the European Cup Winners' Cup semi-final at Elland Road last night.

And it will be very costly for Leeds because Clarke will now be banned automatically from the return in Split in a fortnight.

Clarke reacted angrily to a vicious tackle from behind by Dzoni eighteen minutes from the end, and kicked him.

Hungarian referee Gyula Emsberger said: "I sent off Clarke because he kicked the Yugoslav twice on the thigh."

Leeds will hardly be proud of this performance against a team who defended grimly.

The uncharacteristic traces of anxiety in Leeds' game at the start became more noticeable towards the end.

But manager Don Revie was not despondent. He said: "Naturally we would have liked more goals, but we have been in similar situations before and come out on top."

Surrounded

The goal — Leeds' hundredth this season — was typical of Clarke in his present form.

When the ball reached him after 21 minutes via Johnny Giles and Mick Jones, just inside the penalty area, he was surrounded by three defenders. Yet he left all three stranded and snapped a left-foot drive fiercely and low to the left of goalkeeper Vukcevic.

Kerkh-off in a real storm

RENE van den Kerkhof was sent off as Holland's latest limelight-seekers, Twente Enschede, crashed to a 3—0 defeat in a stormy first leg of their UEFA Cup semi-final with Borussia Muchengladbach in West Germany last night.

Kerkhof got his marching orders three minutes from the end after a foul on Gladbach's brilliant German international Guenter Netzer.

Two goals by Jupp Heynckes and another from Henning Jensen had already put Gladbach well on the way to a final meeting with either Liverpool or Tottenham.

Dino Zoff comfortably collects a ball played into the Juventus box during the 0-0 draw at the Baseball Ground, which was packed to the rafters.

Frank McGhee's despatch from Turin tells of the previous night's disappointment in the foothills of the Italian Alps.

A goalless game at the Baseball Ground a fortnight later meant that, as expected, it was Juventus, not Derby, who claimed their place in the 1973 European Cup final. Alan Hinton missed a penalty and striker Roger Davies, much to his manager's displeasure, was sent off after his temper finally boiled over at Juve's underhand tactics in the second half. Derby actually had the chances to win the game and claim the aggregate victory, but it wasn't to be. The referee for the second leg, Francisco Lobo, told UEFA he had been offered rewards if he favoured Juventus, but UEFA believed the club's defence – that they did not have a relationship with the man alleged to have made the approach. Four years later, the journalist Brian Glanville produced evidence which tied the accused to Juventus in an official capacity. Juventus should have been booted out of the competition that season, with Derby given their place in the final against the Ajax of Johans Cruyff and Neeskens. Who knows where the club would have been now if that had been the case and they had gone on to be crowned champions of Europe?

–LEGENDS–

Alan Hinton

Another of Brian Clough's early signings, Alan Hinton, cost Derby £30,000 from local rivals Nottingham Forest in September 1967. Hinton helped the Rams win the Second Division in his first season at the club, and was a key member of both championship-winning sides. Nicknamed "Gladys" by Derby's fans because of his blond curls and, more so, his refusal to get stuck into tackles in his early days with the club, Hinton finally won them over with his crosses from the left, which were delivered with military precision, and a number of great goals. He was also well known for the white boots he often wore, long before they became fashionable.

FOOTBALL –STATS–

Alan Hinton

Name: Alan Thomas Hinton

Born: 6th October 1942 (Wednesbury)

Playing career: Wolves, Nottm Forest, Derby County, Dallas Tornado, Vancouver Whitecaps

Position: Left-wing

Managerial career: Tulsa Roughnecks, Seattle Sounders, Vancouver Whitecaps, Tacoma Stars, Seattle Sounders

Derby appearances: 316 (1967–75)

Derby goals: 83

England appearances: 3

England goals: 1

A deadly duo

Kevin Hector was already at the club when Brian Clough arrived in 1967 and John O'Hare, a former Sunderland team-mate of the new Derby manager, was his first signing that summer. The £20,000 addition was brought in to be the target man, and Hector would feed to great effect off his lay-offs and knockdowns. O'Hare had very good close control and was as brave as they come. Hector, meanwhile, was all pace, silky skills and a wonderful finisher, and the pair complemented each other superbly.

Arsenal's Sammy Nelson makes a last-ditch challenge on Kevin Hector during a game at Highbury in February 1972.

John O'Hare lets fly against Chelsea (above) and Tottenham (below).

113

The end of an era

Clough had long been at loggerheads with Derby chairman Sam Longson, who did not approve of his manager's TV and newspaper work, and their relationship finally hit rock bottom in October 1973 in the wake of a 1-0 victory at Old Trafford. At the time of that game, certain members of the board had begun asking questions about the role Taylor played at Derby and Longson, for his part, wanted to restrict Clough's media commitments because he was tired of cleaning up the mess he felt his outspoken manager's ways created. Clough, on the other hand, had decided he could no longer work with Longson, and he was even more furious when he found out that his ally's role was under scrutiny. Clough and Longson had a blazing argument on the telephone on the Sunday night, during which the Derby manager resigned on behalf of himself and Taylor. Longson refused to meet that night and instead insisted that the two men offer their written resignations the following morning, which they did. In his autobiography, Clough admitted he had hoped their resignations would be rejected and that they could force Longson out, but that wasn't the case.

Brian Clough exits the Baseball Ground on 16th October 1973 after a meeting with the board and, inset, right-hand man Peter Taylor follows the by-then former Derby manager out of the stadium on a day of high emotion for everyone involved with the club. Clough's work for ITV's *The Big Match* put a real strain on his relationship with chairman Sam Longson.

The victory over Manchester United meant Derby, who were third, with 10 points from seven games, had made their best start to a First Division season under Clough and Taylor. But the departures of the two men plunged the whole club into turmoil, and no one was more bewildered than the players. On 18th October, the Rams stars met with the board after training to discuss the situation, and were later captured by *Mirror* photographer Dick Williams loitering outside the Baseball Ground, talking it through among themselves.

THE DERBY CRISIS

FANS FIGHT FOR CLOUGH

'We'll make board quit and bring back manager'

By DAVE HORRIDGE

DERBY supporters are forming a pressure group to oust the board and restore the Brian Clough-Peter Taylor managerial partnership.

The men leading the move are 42-year-old Bill Holmes, an ex-professional footballer, and Don Shaw, a 39-year-old playwright.

Holmes, now a manager in industry, said yesterday: "Since we announced our plans on the local radio station my phone has not stopped ringing.

"There is a massive demand from Derby supporters for something to be done to get rid of the board and bring back Clough and Taylor.

"We are planning a demo at Saturday's game with Leicester and we intend to hold public meetings to enlist support.

Greatest

"From Derby's average gate of 32,000 we believe that at least 26,000 will support us. We are convinced that if our voice is loud enough, we can put the board out.

"I played under three great managers, at Wolves, Leeds and Doncaster, but for me Brian Clough is the greatest of them all."

Shaw said: "The whole town is seething with anger, and we propose to do all we legally can to get back Clough and Taylor.

"The only way to do that is to get the board to resign."

Club chairman Sam Longson will talk to the Derby players this morning. Then the players will hold their own meeting to discuss the situation.

Jimmy Gordon, the trainer-coach who has been handed temporary charge of the team, insisted last night: "There will be no dressing-room revolt here.

Spirit

"Everyone was upset—myself included—by the resignations of Brian and Peter. But that doesn't mean there will be mass transfer requests.

"The lads know it's got to be a combined effort to pull Derby through.

"I believe they won't allow the team spirit that's been built up to be affected."

But winger Alan Hinton said "We are all terribly disappointed. It's like losing your right arm.

"We grew up with Brian and Peter. They have made us what we are. Wherever they go, the players will want to go with them."

Striker John O'Hare said: "We were playing for Brian and Peter as much as anything. That's why Derby have been successful."

Brian Clough with McFarland and Todd at Wembley.

PLAYBOY!

"They're calling for your resignation, Mr. Chairman and incidentally . . . what's the Vice-Chairman doing there?"

Unsurprisingly, Derby fans were also furious and protests began around the city the day news broke of Clough's departure. A pressure group was quickly set up, which hoped to oust the board and see Clough and Taylor returned to their posts, and the demonstrations continued at the first game following the pair's exit, a clash with East Midlands rivals Leicester on Saturday, 20th October. A march was organized round the area which housed the Baseball Ground and more banners were unfurled inside the stadium. Derby won the game 2-1.

CLOUGH IN DIRECTORS OUT

Feast and Famine
1973-1984

> *To have been managed by Brian Clough, Peter Taylor and Dave Mackay, great people, great characters in this game, who proved their worth. I was pleased to be part of that.*
>
> Roy McFarland

1973 The Rams turn to former fans' favourite Dave Mackay, following the departures of Brian Clough and Peter Taylor, and he steadies the ship, guiding Derby to third in the top flight, which is enough to secure a UEFA Cup spot. **1974** Francis Lee joins from Manchester City and is straight into the European adventure against the likes of Atlético Madrid; Mackay's men are always in and around the leading pack in the First Division and, in another nail-biting end to the campaign, they are crowned champions of England for a second time. **1975–76** Arsenal star Charlie George arrives at the Baseball Ground for £100,000 and makes his debut at Wembley in the Charity Shield against FA Cup winners West Ham; Derby are again on the hunt for European honours, with Real Madrid providing the most glamorous tie of the season. **1976–77** Mackay is sacked in November and replaced by Colin Murphy. **1977–78** The Rams beat Irish side Finn Harps 12-0 in the UEFA Cup to record their biggest victory, with Kevin Hector bagging five goals and Charlie George and Leighton James chipping in with a hat-trick apiece; Ron Webster breaks the club's all-time appearance record when he reaches 526 games; Tommy Docherty replaces Murphy in September. **1979–80** Colin Addison takes over from 'Tommy Doc" and the club are relegated to the Second Division. **1981–82** Kevin Hector scores his 201st and final goal for Derby in his 589th and final game for the club. **1983–84** The threat of extinction hangs over the club in what is a horrible season. A winding-up order in the High Court is lifted but there's still misery when Derby, despite Roy McFarland taking over from Peter Taylor as manager for the last nine games, finish third bottom and are relegated to the Third Division.

Dave Mackay, by then the manager of Nottingham Forest, quickly emerged as the forerunner to replace Clough and, a week later, the club's former skipper was installed. It was a momentous day … and not just in Derby. US president Richard Nixon finally agreed to hand over his White House recordings of the Watergate scandal. As Nixon made front-page news, the Rams' managerial change was the main news item at the back of the paper.

LEFT: Dave Mackay leaves the Baseball Ground during his early days as Derby manager in November 1973.

Mackay holds a dressing-room meeting with his players soon after taking over from Brian Clough, and sits with chairman Sam Longson in the directors' box at Upton Park 10 days after his old boss's departure.

Few players possessed Archie Gemmill's ability to dribble with the ball, and what made his skills even more impressive was the fact he made it look easy on that infamously muddy Baseball Ground pitch. He was another hugely popular player with the crowd and, along with Colin Todd, made the most number of appearances for Derby – 21 – in Europe.

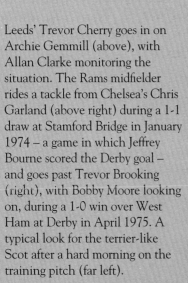

Leeds' Trevor Cherry goes in on Archie Gemmill (above), with Allan Clarke monitoring the situation. The Rams midfielder rides a tackle from Chelsea's Chris Garland (above right) during a 1-1 draw at Stamford Bridge in January 1974 – a game in which Jeffrey Bourne scored the Derby goal – and goes past Trevor Brooking (right), with Bobby Moore looking on, during a 1-0 win over West Ham at Derby in April 1975. A typical look for the terrier-like Scot after a hard morning on the training pitch (far left).

127

Derby's photocall for the 1974–75 campaign. Back row, from left to right: Jimmy Gordon (coach), Colin Todd, Steve Powell, Peter Daniel, Graham Moseley, Colin Boulton, Ron Webster, John O'Hare, John McGovern, Kevin Hector, Des Anderson (assistant-manager/coach). Front row, from left: Henry Newton, Rod Thomas, Bruce Rioch, Roger Davies, Roy McFarland, Dave Mackay, Archie Gemmill, David Nish, Jeff Bourne, Alan Hinton.

129

–LEGENDS–

Colin Boulton

Goalkeeper Colin Boulton was one of only a handful of players to survive a cull when Brian Clough and Peter Taylor arrived in 1967. The Derby manager actually brought in Les Green from Rochdale a year after taking over but, in time, Boulton became his No 1 and would go on to become one of the best stoppers in Derby County history. He was the only ever-present player in both title-winning teams and, in 2009, fans voted him into the goalkeeping spot as they picked the club's all-time XI. Boulton was a police cadet in his hometown of Cheltenham when Rams boss Tim Ward snapped him up in 1964.

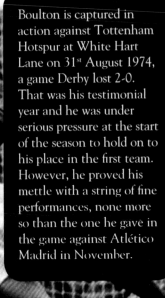

Boulton is captured in action against Tottenham Hotspur at White Hart Lane on 31st August 1974, a game Derby lost 2-0. That was his testimonial year and he was under serious pressure at the start of the season to hold on to his place in the first team. However, he proved his mettle with a string of fine performances, none more so than the one he gave in the game against Atlético Madrid in November.

Derby broke the transfer record in 1972 when they paid Leicester City £225,000 for 21-year-old left-back David Nish. The Burton-born defender, part of the second First Division-winning team, was capped five times by England during his seven years at the Baseball Ground and made 237 appearances for Derby, scoring 14 goals. Here he is pictured trying to block a shot from Stoke's Geoff Hurst in a 1-1 draw at the Victoria Ground on Saturday, 28th September 1974.

FOOTBALL –STATS–

Colin Boulton

Name: Colin Boulton

Born: 12th September 1945 (Cheltenham)

Playing career: Derby County, Southampton (loan), Tulsa Roughnecks, Los Angeles Aztecs, Lincoln City

Position: Goalkeeper

Derby appearances: 344 (1964–77)

SPOT ON!

Derby win on penalties— thanks to cool Colin

COLIN BOULTON, the goalkeeper who said he was playing for his first-team future, ensured Derby's European future with the save of his life.

In a match that illustrated all the drama, excitement, skill and sportsmanship that is rarely seen at this level, he saved the 16th kick of a penalty decider that added tension to the game when there seemed no more room for it.

Derby had survived the shock of a fourth-minute Atletico goal, to go into a second-half lead through Bruce Rioch and Kevin Hector.

Saved

But a late equaliser left the sides level on aggregate at 4—4, and Derby had to drag their tired bodies through 30 minutes of extra time that failed to produce another goal.

Then they faced a five-penalty series before 40,000 excitable Spanish fans in the giant Vicente Calderon stadium.

The unfortunate Roger Davies had his shot

Francis Lee tries to turn the ball past Atletico's goalkeeper Reina during Derby's marathon UEFA Cup battle in Madrid last night.

From
DAVE HORRIDGE in Madrid
Atletico 2, Derby 2 (Agg: 4-4)
Derby win 7-6 on penalties

---

saved. But Bruce Rioch and Kevin Hector had scored before him, while David Nish and Francis Lee were to score after him.

Capon took the next shot after Davies, but put it over the bar. So these two magnificent sides faced a sudden-death decider.

Archie Gemmill, Henry Newton and 19-year-old Steve Powell scored to give Derby a 7—6 lead. Eusebio stepped forward to keep his side in the match.

He put his shot to Boulton's left. But the goalkeeper deflected it against the post, and although Eusebio hit his follow-up shot into the net it didn't count.

Manager Dave Mackay

concede the early goal Mackay had feared.

But their small band of supporters went ecstatic after the two-goal burst inside ten minutes. Rioch got the first after Davies headed down Hector's cross in the 56th minute.

Then the magnificent Lee ended a long run down the right with a pass to Gemmill. His chip into the goalmouth found Hector who volleyed the ball high into the net from twelve yards.

Then Newton was the victim of a harsh free kick decision by West German ref Ferdinand Biwersi and Luis bent the ball into the net from eighteen yards.

Boulton made a tremendous extra-time save from Garate.

Then came the penalty drama

Proud

Mackay said: "This is one of the greatest matches I've been involved in. I have never been more proud of any set of players. They were all magnificent."

Derby left Luis unmarked to head in Adelardo's free kick to

CAN COLIN SAVE HIS FUTURE?

From DAVE HORRIDGE in Madrid

DERBY COUNTY goalkeeper Colin Boulton faces Atletico Madrid here tonight knowing his first team future is at stake.

Boulton, 29, in the middle of his testimonial year, will be under tremendous pressure to hold a Cup-tie as Derby go 2-2 in the first leg, try to go for a win before 70,000 temperamental Spaniards.

But Boulton goes into the match

confident that he can regain the form that earned him the title of 'Mr. Consistency' at Derby, even though he admits he was in danger of being dropped for last Saturday's match at Leeds, following his worst spell in five years of first team football.

Derby beat Leeds 1—0 and Boulton had a blinder. Yesterday Boulton told me: "If I had done anything wrong at Leeds I would not only have been dropped for the Atletico game, I would have asked to have been left out.

"I was playing for my first team future against Leeds and I will be doing the same thing tomorrow. Our reserve keeper Graham Moseley is good enough to stay in the side if he gets the chance."

Derby manager Dave Mackay said: "I have never known any player under such pressure as Colin was at Leeds. He spent an hour on Friday morning convincing me the best place for him to regain confidence was in the first team and not the reserves."

Vital

Derby, minus Colin Todd, face their hardest game against Atletico since drawing 0—0 at Benfica two years ago.

Mackay added: "I am hoping Atletico will think the match is over. We would, in their position.

"The first thirty minutes are vital. It's important for us to score then, but even more important, to stop them scoring.

"Nineteen-year-old Steve Powell takes Todd's place in the back four and Roger Davies plays his first European game of the season.

RIOCH'S RESCUE

By DAVE HORRIDGE
Derby 2, Atl.lco 2

A PENALTY by Bruce Rioch four minutes from time kept Derby's slim UEFA Cup hopes alive last night.

Rioch scored when Francis Lee went down after being tackled by Eusebio.

It was a harsh decision, but no more than Derby deserved after Atletico substitute Luis had scored from a penalty nine minutes earlier when, farcically, keeper Colin Boulton was adjudged to have brought down Garate.

This penalty award to Atletico was the only blemish on French referee Robert Helles performance in a game that thankfully bore no comparison to Atletico's unsavoury display in Glasgow six months ago.

Superb

Ruben Ayala scored first for Atletico but David Nish soon equalised.

Derby got the early goal they wanted in the fifteenth minute through Nish — but Ayala had already beaten them to it.

The great Argentinian gave a superb example of his finishing power when he took a pass from Garate and lashed a 30-yard volley high past Colin Boulton.

The goal Derby needed

to recover from that shock arrived two minutes later when Atletico failed to clear a corner and Nish swept the ball low into the net from fifteen yards.

Despite a tenth minute booking for Benegas for grabbing Kevin Hector's ankle, there was no suggestion of a repeat of the Spaniards' infamous performance against Celtic.

They defended in depth, stubbornly denying Derby's forwards time and space. Shooting chances were rare, although two headers might have produced goals.

When Nish won a

far-post duel with goalkeeper Reina there was nobody waiting for his header when it floated across the empty goal.

Then Henry Newton was unlucky with a low header which slipped past the post.

Derby couldn't afford to concentrate solely on scoring goals with Ayala about. He hit one tremendous left-foot shot just wide, then forced Boulton to an excellent save with a right-foot shot of equal power.

Just before half-time Francis Lee worked a shooting chance for himself and his drive would certainly have troubled Reina if it hadn't been

deflected off Eusebio for a corner.

With thirteen minutes left and the match apparently destined for a draw, Atletico benefited from a ludicrous penalty decision.

When Ron Webster slipped in midfield he left centre-forward Garate through with only Boulton to beat. Boulton timed his dive perfectly but the Atletico striker dived dramatically all over him.

Derby players were stunned when referee Robert Helles pointed to the spot. Atletico delayed the taking of the kick to bring on substitute Luis and he raced on to push the ball i...

Oops! Atletico goalkeeper Reina goes head-over-heels but cannot stop David Nish from shooting home Derby's first-half equaliser.

Portuguese legend Eusébio was back at the Baseball Ground on 24th October 1974, this time with Atlético Madrid, and it proved yet another unhappy evening for the ex-Benfica star. He fouled Francis Lee, giving Bruce Rioch the chance to level matters from the penalty spot and earn Derby a 2-2 draw in the first leg of their second-round encounter. David Nish had scored Derby's first goal. The second leg at the Estadio Vicente Calderón was a massive night for Colin Boulton, who was fighting to prove he was still the Rams' No 1, and he admitted as much to *Mirror* journalist Dave Horridge. But, as the paper reported the following day, Boulton was immense and helped Derby to victory on penalties during a thrilling night in the Spanish capital.

FRANNY FIZZER!

FRANCIS LEE fingered an injured knee and—as if still a Manchester player—asked: "OK if I come in for treatment tomorrow?"

Lee, who lives near Bolton, was assured the Maine Road treatment room would be at his disposal without thought for his sixty-fifth-minute goal which sank his old club.

Lee was delighted about the goal, but more concerned with the stimulating effect it would have on Derby's title prospects than the personal satisfaction involved.

"I don't play for City any more and have to do my best for Derby," he said. "But if we don't win the title I hope City do.

"They put us under a lot of pressure. When City equalised, I expected even more pressure, but we were lucky enough to break away and score again.

Lee's assessment of the situation is accurate enough, though it does not allow for the power he generated in scoring the winning goal nor for the highly organised Derby defence.

Deflected

Which is more than can be said for City's defence when Lee scored.

Three players were virtually within touching distance of him, yet he forced his way through and released a stunning drive beyond goalkeeper Joe Corrigan's reach.

Corrigan reckoned the ball was deflected by Mike Doyle. So did Doyle, who was ungenerous enough to Lee to claim it as an own goal.

But I have no doubt that Franny made it, scored it and is entitled to the glory of it.

There is no doubt either that City could still use him against teams who mount defensive operations, because he would be prepared to risk limb if not life in rushing headlong at them.

Dennis Tueart tried the method, though not often enough, and City were left craving for space without the wit to find it. Crosses pumped hopefully and tiresomely into the middle were their only other weapon.

City were competitive enough, but when there are players like Hadley, Marsh, Colin Bell, Asa Hartford and Joe Royle in the side you look for something more inventive and rewarding than that.

Marsh showed what was needed when he set Bell free for their 63rd minute equaliser, after City had laboured hard to wipe out Henry Newton's 30th minute goal.

Creating space is easier said than done against a defence in which Bruce Rioch, Colin Todd and David Nish were so collaborative.

Doubted

But it is something City must work on because, with such a pathetic away record, they cannot afford to drop points at home.

Derby should not lose too many away if this was a hint of things to come. But I doubt if there will make many friends.

By DEREK WALLIS

Manchester City 1
Derby County 2

Lee flattens his old club —then gets big welcome

Francis Lee . . . delighted with his winner.

Page 30   DAILY MIRROR, Friday, December 6, 1974

Footballer of the Month   FRANCIS LEE Derby County

HAIL THE 'OLD' STAR

By JOHN BEAN

FRANCIS LEE, the chunky Soccer juggernaut for whom life began again at 30, is this Daily Mirror Footballer of the Month for November.

Lee has drummed up all the skill, power and aggression of his Manchester City and England peak since he joined Derby County in August.

And a Derby crowd who have quickly responded to Franny's bounce will see manager Dave Mackay present him with a £100 cheque and an inscribed trophy before the game against Everton tomorrow week.

Filled

The award is just recognition of Lee's efforts to prove himself all over again after seven trophy-filled years at Maine Road.

Franny has already stepped up his personal goal target this season from 15 to 25.

He said yesterday: "I've managed 13 so far —ten in the League—so the original figure looks a bit modest now.

"I honestly think that I'm playing as well as I've ever done.

"Why? It's partly the challenge of proving that at 30 I'm not yet ready for the scrap heap.

"The fans hissed me here whenever I visited the ground with City.

Famous

"All that changed overnight when I joined Derby, now I get along famously with the fans.

"That's why I really appreciate this Daily Mirror award. It's the fans' choice — and if you're pleading them, there can't be much wrong with your game."

Ironically, the award follows Franny's second-half substitution against Velez Mostar in last week's U E F A Cup-tie at Derby and the postponement of Saturday's game.

But typically this complete professional had no qualms about the substitution that eventually broke down the Slav's resistance.

Thirteen goals in the bag already this season . . . and Footballer of the Month Francis Lee is now the idol of the Derby fans.

Francis Lee joined Derby from Manchester City for £100,000 in 1974, and the 12 goals he scored in 34 games during his first season at the club helped the Rams to their second First Division crown. One of those goals came against his old club in an important victory at Maine Road, as the *Mirror* reported on Monday, 30th December 1974. Just a couple of weeks earlier, the newspaper had made Lee Footballer of the Month. The championship medal Lee received that season was his second, as he had already won the title with City during the 1967–68 campaign.

Another local lad, Ripley-born Peter Daniel, came into the world in 1946, the year Derby won the FA Cup, and would go on to join the club as an apprentice before signing professional forms in 1964. His first-team appearances were limited by Roy McFarland, but he still played 246 games in 13 years, after making his debut in 1965. Daniel won the club's Player of the Year award as Derby claimed their second title in 1974–75, when he stood in for the injured McFarland for much of the campaign. Here he heads over Ray Clemence's goal during a 2-0 victory against Liverpool at the Baseball Ground on 11th January 1975. Franny Lee and Henry Newton were on target for the Rams that day.

Roger Davies played in the same game against Liverpool and, while it was Henry Newton and Franny Lee who were on target for Derby that day, the big man from the Black Country scored some very important goals for the club. Davies will perhaps best be remembered for the hat-trick he scored against Tottenham at White Hart Lane on 7th February 1973 in an incredible FA Cup fourth-round replay. Derby were trailing 3-1 with little more than 10 minutes remaining but Davies struck twice to force extra-time, and then completed his treble in the extra period. Kevin Hector, who had given Derby their first lead of the game, wrapped matters up with the Rams' fifth.

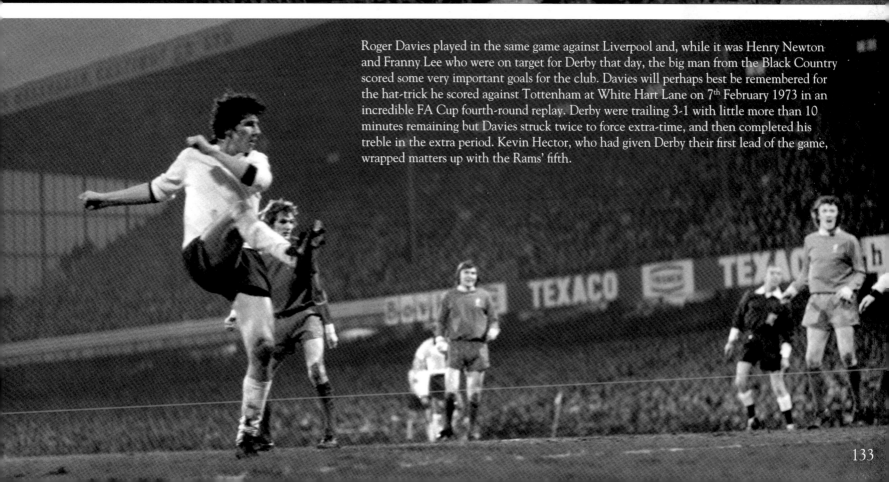

Steve Powell played 420 times for Derby between 1971 and 1984, making 14 more appearances than his dad, Tommy, managed between 1948 and 1961. In this picture, Powell junior (right) can't quite get across to block another fierce shot from Leeds winger Peter Lorimer on 2nd November 1974. Derby won the game 1-0, thanks to a goal from Franny Lee.

Derby didn't, as this picture might suggest, suddenly sell half of the first team to QPR during that 1974–75 campaign; the Rams had just forgotten to pack their away kit for a trip to Loftus Road on 1st February and so had to borrow Rangers' second strip. They soon learned that their hosts' generosity stopped the moment they crossed the white line, with Derby duly given a battering. Bruce Rioch scored their only goal in a 4-1 defeat. Our picture shows Roger Davies, Henry Newton, Archie Gemmill, Rod Thomas and Kevin Hector lining up in a wall. That loss, however, was only a minor blip, and Derby were in the challenging pack as the season turned for home.

135

Hot Toddy

Colin Todd was magnificent in the 1974–75 season, with Peter Daniel alongside him for much of the campaign rather than his usual partner Roy McFarland, who was injured. Todd's form was rewarded by his peers at an awards ceremony at London's Hilton Hotel in March 1975 when the Professional Footballers Association named him Footballer of the Year. He was one of the reasons Derby were flying high in the league with just a handful of games remaining.

Todd, the PFA's Footballer of the Year for the 1974–75 season, is flanked by West Ham goalkeeper Mervyn Day, left, who won Best Young Player, and Denis Law, who was awarded a special prize for Outstanding Services to Football (above). Todd received his trophy from Prime Minister Harold Wilson (right).

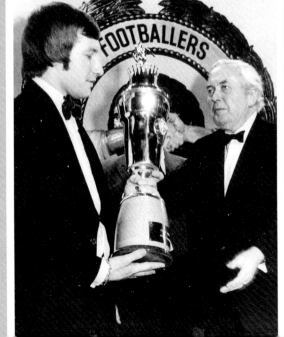

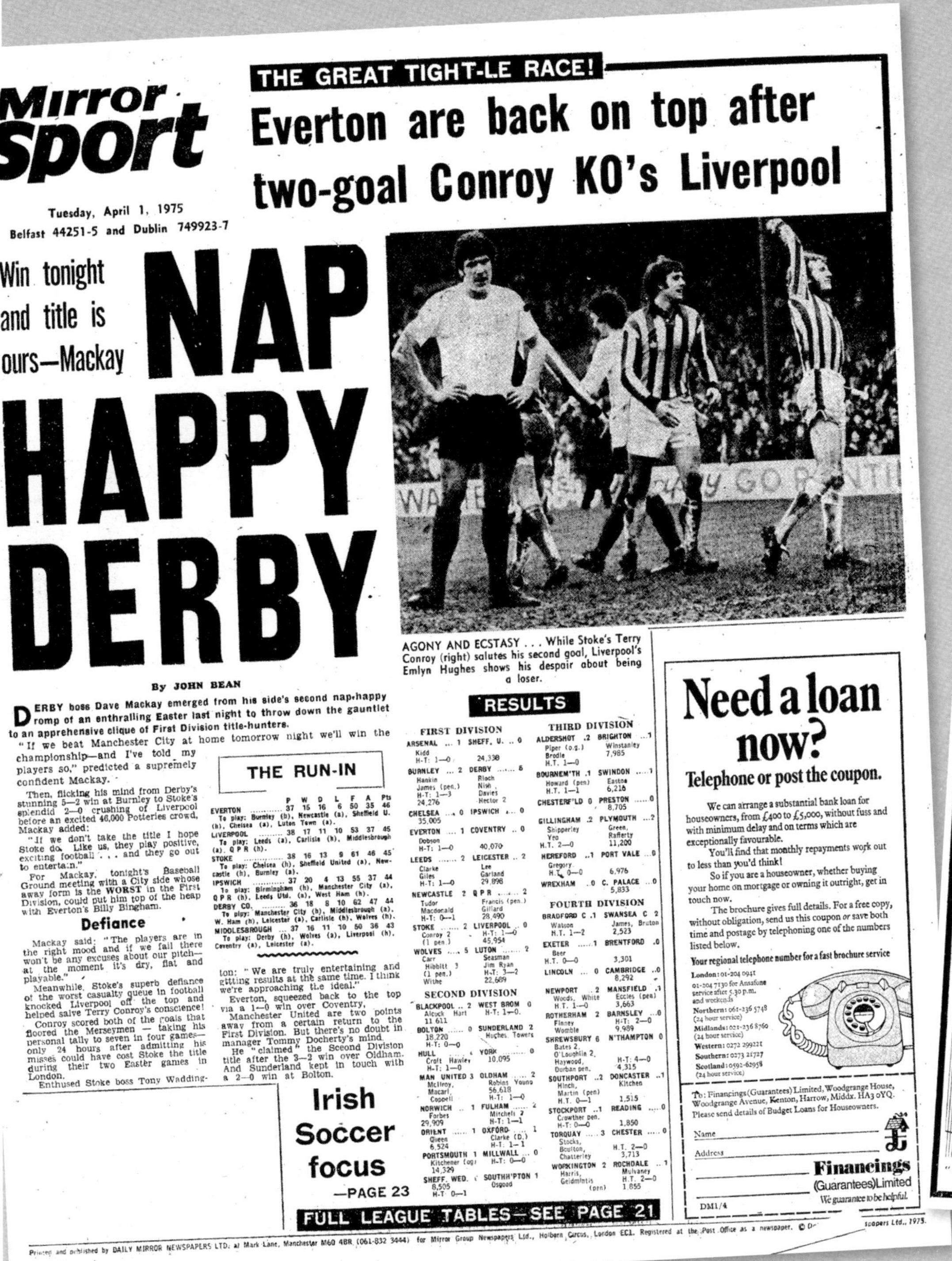

THE GREAT TIGHT-LE RACE!

Everton are back on top after two-goal Conroy KO's Liverpool

Mirror Sport

Tuesday, April 1, 1975
Belfast 44251-5 and Dublin 749923-7

Win tonight and title is ours—Mackay

NAP HAPPY DERBY

AGONY AND ECSTASY . . . While Stoke's Terry Conroy (right) salutes his second goal, Liverpool's Emlyn Hughes shows his despair about being a loser.

By JOHN BEAN

DERBY boss Dave Mackay emerged from his side's second nap-happy romp of an enthralling Easter last night to throw down the gauntlet to an apprehensive clique of First Division title-hunters.

"If we beat Manchester City at home tomorrow night we'll win the championship—and I've told my players so," predicted a supremely confident Mackay.

Then, flicking his mind from Derby's stunning 5—2 win at Burnley to Stoke's splendid 2—0 crushing of Liverpool before an excited 46,000 Potteries crowd, Mackay added:

"If we don't take the title I hope Stoke do. Like us, they play positive, exciting football . . . and they go out to entertain."

For Mackay, tonight's Baseball Ground meeting with a City side whose away form is the **WORST** in the First Division, could put him top of the heap with Everton's Billy Bingham.

Defiance

Mackay said: "The players are in the right mood and if we fail there won't be any excuses about our pitch—at the moment it's dry, flat and playable."

Meanwhile, Stoke's superb defiance of the worst casualty queue in football knocked Liverpool off the top and helped salve Terry Conroy's conscience!

Conroy scored both of the goals that floored the Merseymen — taking his personal tally to seven in four games—only 24 hours after admitting his misses could have cost Stoke the title during their two Easter games in London.

Enthused Stoke boss Tony Waddington: "We are truly entertaining and getting results at the same time. I think we're approaching the ideal."

Everton, squeezed back to the top via a 1—0 win over Coventry.

Manchester United are two points away from a certain return to the First Division. But there's no doubt in manager Tommy Docherty's mind.

He "claimed" the Second Division title after the 3—2 win over Oldham. And Sunderland kept in touch with a 2—0 win at Bolton.

THE RUN-IN

	P	W	D	L	F	A	Pts
EVERTON	37	15	16	6	50	35	46
To play: Burnley (h), Newcastle (a), Sheffield U. (h), Chelsea (a), Luton Town (a).							
LIVERPOOL	38	17	11	10	53	37	45
To play: Leeds (a), Carlisle (h), Middlesbrough (a), Q P R (h).							
STOKE	38	16	13	9	61	46	45
To play: Chelsea (h), Sheffield United (a), Newcastle (h), Burnley (a).							
IPSWICH	37	20	4	13	55	37	44
To play: Birmingham (h), Manchester City (a), Q P R (h), Leeds Utd. (a), West Ham (h).							
DERBY CO.	36	18	8	10	62	47	44
To play: Manchester City (h), Middlesbrough (a), W. Ham (h), Leicester (a), Carlisle (h), Wolves (h).							
MIDDLESBROUGH	37	16	11	10	50	36	43
To play: Derby (h), Wolves (a), Liverpool (h), Coventry (a), Leicester (a).							

RESULTS

FIRST DIVISION

ARSENAL ... 1 (Kidd; H-T: 1—0) SHEFF. U. .. 0 — 24,338
BURNLEY ... 2 (Hankin, James (pen.); H-T: 1—3; 24,276) DERBY ...... 5 (Rioch, Nish, Davies, Hector 2)
CHELSEA ... 0 (35,005) IPSWICH ... 0
EVERTON .... 1 (Dobson; H-T: 1—0) COVENTRY .. 0 — 40,070
LEEDS .... 2 (Clarke, Giles; H-T: 1—0) LEICESTER .. 2 (Lee, Garland; 29,898)
NEWCASTLE 2 (Tudor, Macdonald; H-T: 0—1) Q P R .... 2 (Francis (pen.), Gillard; 28,490)
STOKE .... 2 (Conroy 2 (1 pen.)) LIVERPOOL .. 0 (H-T: 1—0; 45,954)
WOLVES .... 5 (Carr, Hibbitt 3 (1 pen.), Withe) LUTON .... 2 (Seasman, Jim Ryan; H-T: 3—2; 22,689)

SECOND DIVISION

BLACKPOOL .. 2 (Alcock, Hart; 11,611) WEST BROM 0 (H-T: 1—0.)
BOLTON ...... 0 (18,220; H-T: 0—0) SUNDERLAND 2 (Hughes, Towers)
HULL .... (Croft, Hawley; H-T: 1—0) YORK 0 (10,095)
MAN UNITED 3 (McIlroy, Macari, Coppell) OLDHAM ..... 2 (Robins, Young; 56,618; H-T: 1—0)
NORWICH .. 1 (Forbes; 29,909) FULHAM ...... 2 (Mitchell 2; H-T: 1—1)
ORIENT ...... 1 (Queen; 6,524) OXFORD ..... 1 (Clarke (D.); H-T: 1—1)
PORTSMOUTH 1 (Kitchener (og); 14,329) MILLWALL ... 0 (H-T: 0—0)
SHEFF. WED. ((8,505; H-T 0—1) SOUTHH'PTON 1 (Osgood)

THIRD DIVISION

ALDERSHOT .2 (Piper (o.g.), Brodie; H.T. 1—0) BRIGHTON ...1 (Winstanley; 7,985)
BOURNEM'TH .1 (Howard (pen); H.T. 1—1) SWINDON .....1 (Eastoe; 6,216)
CHESTERF'LD 0 PRESTON 0 (8,705)
GILLINGHAM .2 (Shipperley, Yeo; H.T. 2—0) PLYMOUTH ...2 (Green, Rafferty; 11,200)
HEREFORD ..1 (Gregory; H.T. 0—0) PORT VALE ...0 (6,976)
WREXHAM ..0 C. PALACE ...0 (5,833)

FOURTH DIVISION

BRADFORD C .1 (Watson; H.T. 1—2) SWANSEA C 2 (James, Bruton; 2,523)
EXETER ......1 (Beer; H.T. 0—0) BRENTFORD .0 (3,301)
LINCOLN ... 0 CAMBRIDGE ..0 (8,292)
NEWPORT ..2 (Woods, White; H.T. 1—0) MANSFIELD .1 (Eccles (pen); 3,663)
ROTHERHAM 2 (Finney, Womble) BARNSLEY ...0 (H-T: 2—0; 9,989)
SHREWSBURY 6 (Bates 2, O'Loughlin 2, Haywood, Durban pen.) N'THAMPTON 0 (H-T: 4—0; 4,315)
SOUTHPORT ..2 (Hinch, Martin (pen); H.T. 0—1) DONCASTER ..1 (Kitchen; 1,515)
STOCKPORT ..1 (Crowther pen.; H-T: 0—0) READING 0 (1,850)
TORQUAY ....3 (Stocks, Boulton, Chatterley) CHESTER .....0 (H.T. 2—0; 3,713)
WORKINGTON 2 (Harris, Geidmintis (pen)) ROCHDALE ...1 (Mulvaney; H.T. 2—0; 1,855)

Irish Soccer focus

—PAGE 23

FULL LEAGUE TABLES—SEE PAGE 21

Need a loan now?
Telephone or post the coupon.
We can arrange a substantial bank loan for houseowners, from £400 to £5,000, without fuss and with minimum delay and on terms which are exceptionally favourable.
You'll find that monthly repayments work out to less than you'd think!
So if you are a houseowner, whether buying your home on mortgage or owning it outright, get in touch now.
The brochure gives full details. For a free copy, without obligation, send us this coupon or save both time and postage by telephoning one of the numbers listed below.
Your regional telephone number for a fast brochure service
London: 01-204 0941
01-204 7130 for Ansafone service after 5.30 p.m. and weekends
Northern: 061-236 5748 (24 hour service)
Midlands: 021-236 8760 (24 hour service)
Western: 0272 299221
Southern: 0273 21727
Scotland: 0592-62958 (24 hour service)
To: Financings (Guarantees) Limited, Woodgrange House, Woodgrange Avenue, Kenton, Harrow, Middx. HA3 0YQ.
Please send details of Budget Loans for Houseowners.
Name
Address
DM1/4
Financings (Guarantees) Limited
We guarantee to be helpful.

Printed and published by DAILY MIRROR NEWSPAPERS LTD. at Mark Lane, Manchester M60 4BR (061-832 3444) for Mirror Group Newspapers Ltd., Holborn Circus, London EC1. Registered at the Post Office as a newspaper. © D... spapers Ltd., 1975.

FRANK McGHEE THE VOICE OF SPORT talks to Dave Mackay, the man who's got the bubbly on ice..

They've earned the right to be champions

DERBY manager Dave Mackay was content, after the goalless draw at Leicester, to let other people work out that his team could still finish runners-up in the championship.

Mackay's lively mind already was ranging far ahead. "We'll win the First Division again even easier next season," he says, discounting any possibility of being overhauled on the finishing line this time.

"We will be a year more experienced, more mature. Already we have the strongest, best squad in the business and next year we'll have one more player." Mackay isn't saying who, but the popular bet is that his target is Duncan McKenzie, of Leeds.

Coming down to earth and back to the present, Mackay is convinced the championship will be decided at Manchester City's ground on Wednesday. "Ipswich will lose there and fall too far behind to catch us."

I asked him whether he wouldn't prefer to win it in the grand style, in front of Derby's own fans in the final match next Saturday against Carlisle. Because, no matter what miracles Ipswich produce, one more point would make Derby's position impregnable.

DAVE MACKAY
'We'll do it again next year.'

Disappointing

"No, Wednesday will suit us fine," he grinned. "We have the champagne on ice already."

Looking back on a disappointing Leicester match, I asked Dave if he didn't regret that his team, one of the rare advocates of adventure, had failed to finish it.

Instead, for the last fifteen minutes, Derby lapsed into the depressingly familiar fashion set by too many others this season, dropping back, wasting time, playing a possession game.

"Fifteen minutes of defensive football in a season isn't bad," said Mackay. "And of course I don't regret it. It was the right thing to do to get the point. That was all we ever expected."

Another explanation for Derby's uncharacteristic timidity came from their most experienced player, Francis Lee.

This veteran buccaneer said: "The tension was terrible, even for me. I found myself doing all the wrong things, chasing the ball like a schoolboy when, out of the whole team, I'm the one who should have known better.

"However long you've been in the game you still can't help suffering at times like this. But you don't win a championship on one day. Nine months of work decide whether you deserve it—and Derby deserve it."

No argument there. The fifteen minutes of pure flowing football the champions-elect supplied at the start contained everything they have produced in this final surge which has taken them to the top with fourteen out of sixteen possible points, six wins and two draws.

From midfield the tricky little Gemmill and the elegant, powerful Rioch were feeding the urgency of Lee, the dangerous gallops of Davies. Leicester were being delicately dismantled rather than destroyed.

Discretion

Davies might have had a couple and Rioch, who hits the ball as though he hates it, could have made himself a candidate for the goal of the season in this spell.

But when a couple of Leicester counter-attacks reached as far as near-miss shots by centre-forward Frank Worthington, Derby decided to settle for discretion rather than valour—and, in a different way, underlined another aspect of their credentials for Europe next season.

Colin Todd, abandoning attacking thrusts, dropped back to take such effective control of his penalty area that centre half Roy McFarland was able to claim afterwards Derby were never in the slightest danger of losing.

Full backs David Nish and Rod Thomas had masterly matches. The impression they all created was of men in complete charge of a situation.

They have established their right to be champions

PLAYBOY!

"Only one more week of tension, boss, and then you can start to relax!"

With six games to go and the club chasing their second First Division crown, confidence was high in Derby, particularly with manager Dave Mackay. He told his boys through the *Mirror* on Tuesday, 1st April 1975, that they would win the title if they beat Manchester City at the Baseball Ground that night – and they duly obliged with a 2-1 win, courtesy of a Bruce Rioch double. Four games later, Derby were held to a goalless draw by Leicester, but Ipswich, Liverpool and Everton all lost, to hand the initiative to the Rams. That meant Derby needed to take just a point from their game against Carlisle the following week, their last outing of the season, to win the title, even though the Tractor Boys still had two games to play.

Champions again

A midweek slip-up by Ipswich, who could only manage a draw against Manchester City, meant Derby could not be caught at the top of the table, and that the game against Carlisle was just a formality. Derby drew the match 0-0 but the party had already started at the Baseball Ground. Liverpool finished second, with Ipswich third, both clubs on 51 points, two behind Derby.

Derby were presented with the First Division trophy ahead of their game with Carlisle on 26th April 1975 and show off their silverware as they salute the Baseball Ground crowd on a lap of honour after the game.

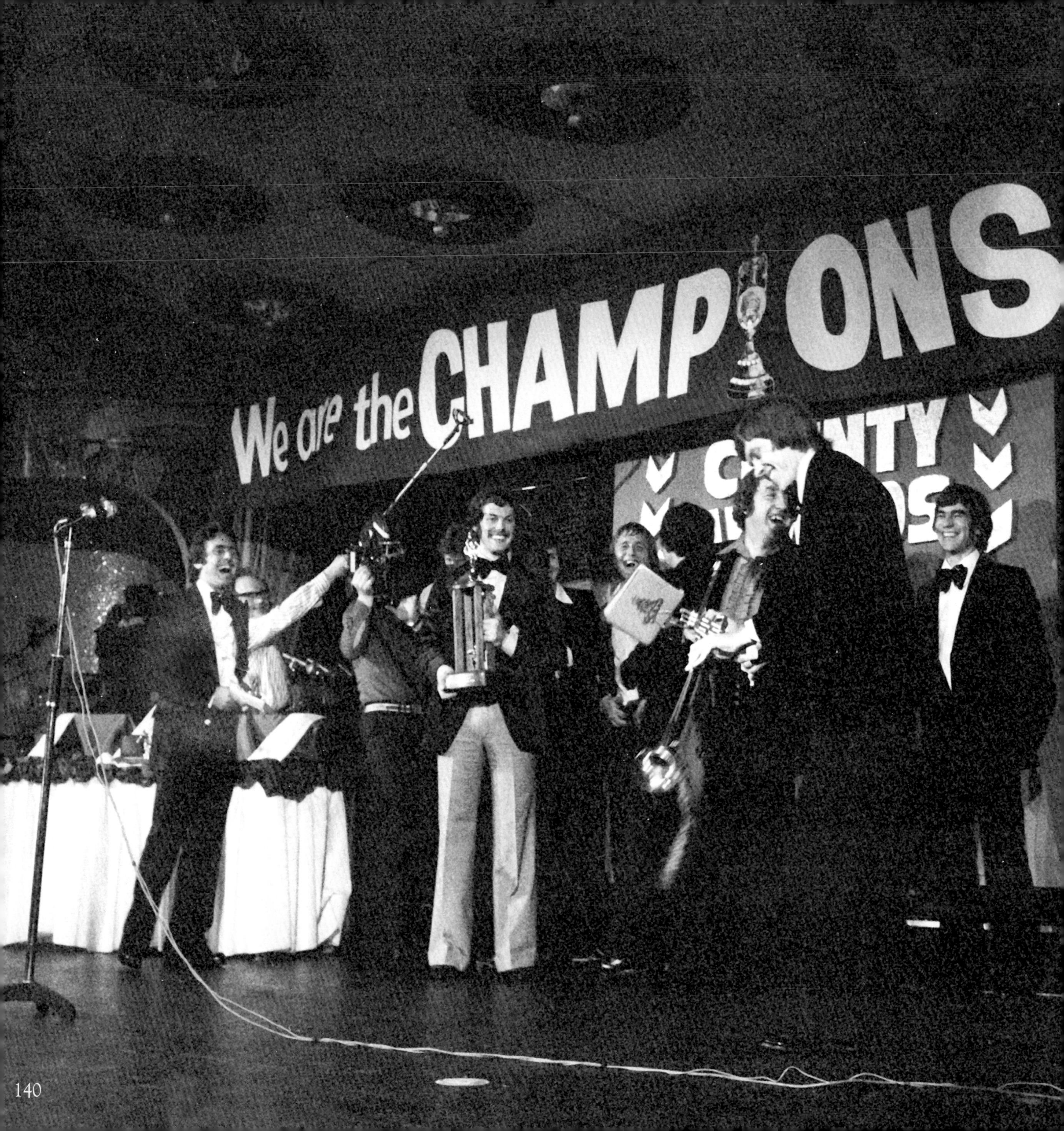
We are the CHAMP ONS

The banner says it all as Derby celebrate their triumph. Above, assistant-manager Des Anderson toasts the Rams' success with players Henry Newton, Rod Thomas and Francis Lee while, below, Roger Davies looks on amused as David Nish empties a bottle of bubbly over Peter Daniel.

The Rams stars descended on Majorca once again to celebrate their title success. There was plenty of time for soaking up the sun with a shift on the beach ... and even more time to sink a few celebratory pints at The Red Lion.

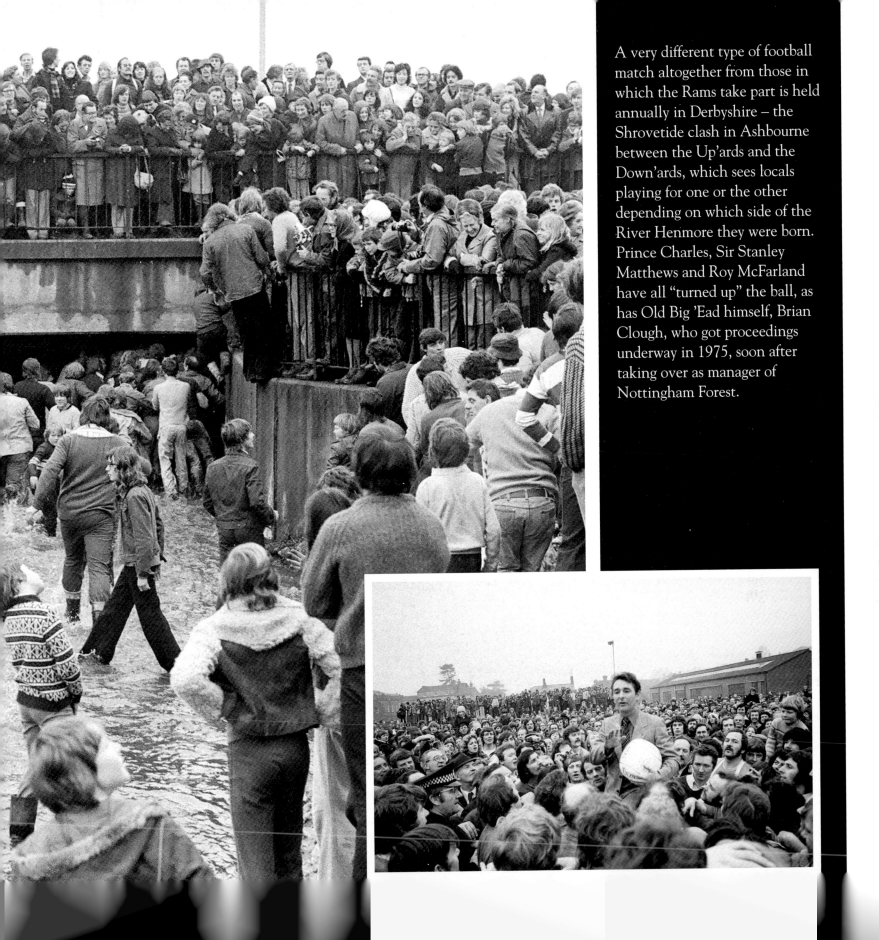

A very different type of football match altogether from those in which the Rams take part is held annually in Derbyshire – the Shrovetide clash in Ashbourne between the Up'ards and the Down'ards, which sees locals playing for one or the other depending on which side of the River Henmore they were born. Prince Charles, Sir Stanley Matthews and Roy McFarland have all "turned up" the ball, as has Old Big 'Ead himself, Brian Clough, who got proceedings underway in 1975, soon after taking over as manager of Nottingham Forest.

As champions, Derby took part in the traditional curtain-raiser to the season, the Charity Shield, the following August, and got off to a winning start in the campaign with a 2-0 victory over FA Cup winners, West Ham, at Wembley. Kevin Hector and Roy McFarland scored for Dave Mackay's side. Charlie George had signed for Derby that summer, with Mackay making sure he put pen to paper at a London hotel. George, who is also pictured getting into his car after leaving that meeting with Mackay, made his debut against the Hammers at the famous old stadium.

147

148

Derby's central-defensive duo, Roy McFarland and Colin Todd, were both 20-something cap winners with England. *Mirror* photographer Monte Fresco snapped the pair larking about in their hotel room after reporting for Three Lions duty ahead of the 1976 European Championship qualifier against Czechoslovakia in October 1975. Three years earlier, the pair had celebrated Derby's first title triumph with a cup of tea each in the room they were sharing on international duty, after leaving their team-mates in Spain to join up with the rest of the England squad.

Real Madrid goalkeeper Miguel Ángel saves at the feet of Francis Lee in one of the most memorable matches at the Baseball Ground (left). The Rams had already beaten Slovan Bratislava, then a part of Czechoslovakia, in the first round – the above picture shows Derby players celebrating the 3-0 home victory in the second leg of that tie while the *Mirror* reports the 1-0 win in the first leg – and they duly sent Spanish giants Real packing, with a 4-1 victory in the first leg of the second round. There was political unrest in Spain at the time and concerns were raised about the welfare of Derby's players and fans ahead of their visit to the Bernabéu. At the Baseball Ground, however, there were no such worries, and the atmosphere that night was electric. A Charlie George double, the second from the penalty spot, put Derby two up before José Martínez Sánchez, better known in the Seventies as Pirri, pulled a goal back for the visitors. Nish then restored Derby's two-goal advantage before George bagged another from the spot in the second half to complete his hat-trick and cap a wonderful night in the East Midlands. Dave Mackay and his men were on course to claim the biggest scalp in Derby's history … but an even more remarkable and dramatic night was to follow in Madrid a fortnight later.

Mirror Sport

 **BATTLE IN EUROPE**

Thursday, October 23, 1975
Telephone: (STD code 01)—353 0246

Hammers robbed in Russia
PAGE 31

Ipswich slam three
PAGE 30

GEORGE-OUS!

DERBY provided something to shout about. Real Madrid were left with plenty to complain about.

That, in a paragraph, is the summary of this European Cup game.

A game in which the English champions provided the three-goal lead manager Dave Mackay had demanded as a virtual guarantee of their progress into the quarter-finals.

Charlie George, inspiring and inspired, was in unforgettable form, the most eye-catching performer on the field. Colin Todd was implacable, unbeatable in defence.

Archie Gemmill dominated a midfield that contained two great Germans—Gunter Netzer and Paul Breitner—which says all there is to say about the little Scot.

That, in another paragraph, provides the basic reason why Derby deserved the margin of a marvellous and memorable victory.

But I still can't blame the Real Madrid players for the scowling bitterness on their faces at the end.

Referee Ivanov shrugs off angry Madrid protests . . . and Charlie George is congratulated by Archie Gemmill (right) after completing a hat-trick from the spot. *Pictures: MONTE FRESCO*

Penalty rumpus as Charlie floors Real with hat-trick

By FRANK McGHEE

Derby 4
Real Madrid . . 1

Protests

Derby scored two of their goals from penalties—both slammed in by the ice-cool George—the second of which was hotly disputed.

Real were denied one penalty they felt was justified, and also had a goal disallowed for an offside decision which they queried almost as fiercely.

What they cannot question or dispute, however, was Derby's total superiority on a night of magnificent football.

It was George who began it all in the tenth minute with a goal as sweetly struck as any I have ever seen.

The ball came to him hard and low from Gemmill on the left, a difficult chance that in an instant became a volley of ferocious power.

By the fifteenth minute it was 2—0, with George slamming home a penalty after Francis Lee had been tripped.

But Madrid always remained capable of devastating counter-punching through striker Martinez, and his agile, veteran partner Amancio.

It was Amancio who laid on the twenty-fifth minute goal that put Madrid back in the game. His cross created

all the time and room Pirri needed to place his shot.

It was at this stage that Madrid were denied a penalty which could have dragged them undeservedly level. Russian referee Ivanov decided that the Rod Thomas tackle which felled Martinez connected inches outside the area.

There were, however, no complaints from manager Miljan Miljanic, who sportingly—and truthfully—preferred to praise Derby's quality.

Thump

Derby went 3—1 up just before half-time when centre half Roy McFarland charged upfield to give David Nish the chance to thump the ball in from outside the penalty area.

It was keeper Angel's error, but he was able to atone at least half-a-dozen times with brilliant saves in the second half.

I felt sorry for Madrid only once—in the 65th minute—when Pirri slotted the ball home brilliantly, only to be given offside.

Derby's fourth goal came in the 77th minute when George scored his second penalty and completed his hat-trick—with Madrid complaining bitterly about the award of the spot-kick for a tackle by Netzer on Kevin Hector.

A wonderful night at the Baseball Ground saw Charlie George's hat-trick quite rightly create the following morning's headlines after he had given Derby a first-leg advantage.

Mirror Sport

BATTLE IN EUROPE

SKY-HIGH HAMMERS
Pages 30 and 31
IPSWICH SHATTERED
Page 31

BE A WINNER IN THE MIRROR

FOUR NAPS IN A ROW!

DICK RATCLIFF landed his FOURTH successive nap yesterday, when Paper Chase won at 2—1. He also gave Sea Pigeon 7—2 for two winners out of three. TIM RICHARDS, back from holiday, napped Fugal Deal 7—4 to take his nap profit to more than £34 to a £1 stake. He also gave Contabet 5—4. BOUVERIE'S nine winners included Wrongly Down 100-30, Posidon 11-4, Lyon Del Mar 5-2, Fugal Deal, Chosen Slave 11-8 and Contabet.

THE WINNING RACING MIRROR—Pages 28, 29.

Thursday, November 6, 1975

INCREDIBLE!

Derby crash out as Real smash five to clinch it in extra time

IT IS barely believable that Derby are out of the European Cup.

It is incredible that the three-goal lead they built so brilliantly in the first leg of the second round match was smashed in the Bernabeau Stadium in Madrid last night.

Something special had to happen to cause it. And something special did—a performance by the Spanish champions which revived memories of this great club's most golden days.

Some Derby players were, understandably, muttering bitterly afterwards about the penalty award in the 84th minute which sent the match into extra time.

That ordeal for their tired limbs made it virtually certain they would lose—because few English sides have ever gone to a foreign field in a worse state than Derby.

Two key players, midfield man Henry Newton and centre half Roy McFarland, were walking-wounded. Charlie George, their Cockney striker, spent the day in bed with a stomach upset and a sore throat.

These, however, are explanations rather than excuses — because McFarland, tenacious and tough, was Derby's outstanding player and George their only goal.

But this is a story that demands to be told as it unfolded against the towering, screaming stands of the stadium in a hot and hostile atmosphere.

Derby could not have made a worse start, losing the first of their precious three-goal lead within three minutes.

The goal was set up by the brilliant German, Gunther Netzer, and forced in by Martinez.

Throughout the rest of the first half Derby were outclassed as comprehensively as they outshone Real in the first leg.

They must have felt

Derby's Roy McFarland leaps to challenge Roberto as Real Madrid's two-goal hero, Santillana (left) waits to pounce.

From FRANK McGHEE
Real Madrid 5, Derby 1
(Agg: Real win 6—5 after extra time)

they were facing the Chinese infantry as waves of non-stop attacks came pouring in and they didn't have a single worthwhile one of their own to recall during the haven of half-time.

Menace

As well as Netzer, the little Madrid winger Amancio was full of wriggling, spiteful menace. Pirri, who combines the job of sweeping with that of striking, provided a memorable display.

Martinez, tall, strong and dangerous, created constant danger.

Derby's hope seemed to have died in the ten minutes after half-time. Real pulled back an-

other goal in the fiftieth minute following an Amancio free kick. Goalkeeper Colin Boulton did well to parry Santillana's header and even better to block the centre forward's second attempt.

But he was left stranded as Martinez rammed a shot into the corner of the net.

Now Real were only one goal away from outright victory — and that goal arrived just five minutes later.

Netzer used his size eleven boot to curl a free kick across the penalty area and Santillana soared to score with a superb header.

The 4—1 scoreline from the first leg had become 4—4 and the goal Real

had scored in Derby put them in front.

But the pattern of the game changed immediately. Real fell back to protect their slender advantage and Derby pushed forward.

Real Madrid have never made a bigger mistake. Their caution cost them a goal in the 62nd minute.

Tense

Snapping up a short ball from McFarland, George weaved an intricate path through two tackles across the edge of the penalty area before unleashing a right-foot shot that hit the underside of the bar and dropped down a foot over the line.

That put Derby in front again and created a terribly tense situation. Swiss referee Hungercusher denied Real a succession of penalty claims.

But though Derby

hotly disputed the award he gave in the 84th minute he was right on the spot to decide that Rod Thomas had tripped Amancio.

Pirri made it 4-1 from the spot—the same score as in the first leg—and sent the game into extra time.

In the tenth minute of extra time strong man Paul Breitner sent Santillana in to lift the ball over David Nish's head and run round him to drive home his shot.

Two minutes later Derby's only really fit and fresh man, substitute Jeff Bourne, collapsed after a tackle with Camacho and was carried off with badly damaged cartilage.

I can only end by agreeing with Derby manager Dave Mackay when he said: "We played them off the park at our ground. They did the same to us tonight."

WREXHAM the Third Division club without an away League point this season, secured a place in the quarter-finals of the European Cup Winners' Cup last night.

The Welsh club went to Poland and drew 1—1 with Stal Rzeszow to go through 3—1 on aggregate and join Celtic and West Ham in the last eight.

These three salvaged some British pride on a night of shock defeats.

Sadly Derby, Ipswich, Dundee United and little Athlone Town all waved farewell to Europe.

European Cup holders Bayern Munich, starting one down from their first

Wrexham's night of Cup glory

leg in Sweden, won through to the quarter-finals by beating Malmoe 2—0 with a penalty from Duernberger and a goal from Torstensson.

The French side St. Etienne, the only other survivor from last season's European Cup semi-finals, scored a fine 2—1 win over Rangers in Glasgow to qualify on a 4—1 aggregate.

● The Spanish champions restored memories of their most golden days ●

Printed and Published by THE DAILY MIRROR NEWSPAPERS Ltd. (01-353 0246) at, and for Mirror Group Newspapers Ltd., Holborn Circus, London, E C1P 1DQ. Registered at the Post Office as a newspaper.

© The Daily Mirror Newspapers Ltd., 1975.

"Incredible", however, was perhaps the only word which headline writers could use a couple of weeks later to adequately sum up what happened in the replay in Madrid on Bonfire Night, 1975, as Real sealed a 6-5 aggregate victory over Derby with an explosive performance. Roberto Juan Martínez and Santillana scored twice for Real, with Pirri also on target. Charlie George hit the Rams' only goal of the game.

The BBC's Clash of the Day

Between those two encounters with Real Madrid, Derby still had plenty to play for on the home front, and clashes with Leeds, particularly during the late Sixties and Seventies, always caught the nation's attention. Unsurprisingly, the BBC's *Match of the Day* programme sent its cameras to the Baseball Ground for a First Division clash on 1st November, hoping for another humdinger between the two sides – and what a great decision it proved, with viewers treated to a real dust-up between Francis Lee and Norman Hunter. It would go on to become one of the show's most famous pieces of footage and is still recalled as one of football's best brawls to this day. The pair had been bickering for some time after Lee won a penalty for Derby, with the Leeds No 6 unhappy with the way he won it, and they continued to exchange words until eventually the red mist descended on both. Hunter landed a huge punch on Lee, which made a real mess of his mouth, although team-mates got in-between the warring pair before the fight really got going. Lee, however, was still seething as the two of them, having both been sent off, left the field and he launched a frenzied attack on Hunter. Swinging wildly, Lee didn't appear to actually land a blow as Hunter backed off and, as the Leeds man tripped, players from both sides again dived between them, with some even trying to restore order. Eventually Gordon Guthrie, the much-loved Rams physio, and manager Dave Mackay were able to escort the bloodied Lee off the pitch, but he still had to be restrained in the home dressing room and prevented from heading back down the tunnel to the visitors' room. The scoreline was almost lost among the mayhem but Derby won 3-2. Charlie George converted the penalty Lee had won, while Archie Gemmill added the second for the Rams and Roger Davies the third.

WAGs, Seventies style ...

Leighton James and wife Ann pose at their new home while, above right, Jean Lee looks adoringly at her husband Francis; above far right, Archie Gemmill plays the family man with wife Betty, son Scot, who would play for Nottingham Forest and Scotland, and daughter Stacey; and, opposite, Colin Todd signs autographs as he arrives at the Baseball Ground to complete his move to Derby with wife Jenny by his side.

157

Mirror Sport

Friday, November 26, 1976
Telephone: (STD code 01)—353 0246

CHANNEL ISLANDS 7p

Vote of confidence? Sorry Dave, say Derby directors..

YOU'RE FIRED!

Grim-faced Dave Mackay drives out of his job as Derby manager after last night's dramatic sacking.

Ormond ready to quit

By JAMES SANDERSON

SCOTLAND team boss Willie Ormond is on the verge of quitting.

I can reveal that after weeks of waiting, Ormond has received a new offer of a new contract from the Scottish Football Association.

It was delivered to his home yesterday, and close friends told me: "Willie is fuming—he does not consider the terms to be fair at all."

The Scotland boss, deeply involved in World Cup qualifying games against Czechoslovakia and Wales, would not comment, except to tell me: "I have received an offer.

"I shall be replying to the SFA at the weekend. I have nothing more to say."

Ormond, who took Scotland through the 1974 World Cup undefeated and this year won the British home championship, is due to have his £7,500-a-year contract renewed at the end of December.

Waiting in the wings is whizz-kid Andy Roxburgh, the university graduate who is now national director of coaching

SPOT ON

TOPSPOT (the Spotform nap) gave The Clerk 9-4 yesterday.

The winning Racing Mirror—Pages 28, 29

By DAVID MOORE

DAVE MACKAY demanded a vote of confidence from Derby County's five directors last night—and got the sack instead.

Not a single hand went up in his favour . . . and that signalled the end of a 37-month reign at the Baseball Ground that turned sour for manager Mackay and his assistant Des Anderson.

Durban tipped to take over

There will be no immediate appointment of a successor, although names linked with the vacancy are sure to include Alan Durban and Brian Clough.

The shock waves of Clough's resignation in September, 1973, are still felt in the town and there could now be a strong body of public opinion calling for an approach to Nottingham Forest to secure his release.

Success

Durban, the former Derby player who is making a success of his first managerial post at Shrewsbury, has been consistently tipped to take over from Mackay.

In reply to Mackay's demand for a confidence vote, Derby issued a statement which said: "The board were reluctantly unable to give Mr. Mackay any assurance and it was decided to relinquish the manager and his assistant

of their duties forthwith."

Sam Longson, earlier elected life president which means George Hardy is set to take over as chairman, added that although Mackay was not under contract there had been "a financial arrangement" with the manager.

Reserve coach Colin Murphy takes over as caretaker and he immediately joined Mackay and Anderson behind locked doors to arrange an orderly transfer of power.

Then 40-year-old Mackay emerged to walk to his car pausing only to declare: "Obviously I hope to stay in football —and I expect to do so. I did all my talking in there."

Anderson would add only: "The sack is an occupational hazard."

They have paid the price for Derby's lack of success this season following failure to push home their challenge for the championship last season after defeat by Manchester United in the FA Cup semi-finals.

No Rush

The £310,000 signing of winger Leighton James has brought little but criticism and England defender Colin Todd had to be placated with promises of an improved contract after asking for a transfer.

It is Murphy's task to restore the spirit of a side with only two wins in thirteen League games

ALAN DURBAN . . . return to Derby?

Hardy, the strong man in Derby's boardroom, said: "There will be no speedy appointment and I expect Colin Murphy to stay in charge until the end of the year.

"It was a cards-on-the-table situation with Dave Mackay.

"People might think we have acted hastily with only a third of the season gone, but if a choice of alternatives is offered you can't be surprised if things go against you.

"If you are manager of a top-class team and don't get results the job isn't there for ever."

Leighton James said: "I am shocked and disappointed by what has happened."

'LIVING ON A KNIFE-EDGE..'

By KEVIN MOSELEY

KEITH BURKINSHAW, manager of a Tottenham side chasing a point-a-game target to avoid relegation, spoke last night about "living on a knife-edge."

And the man who has been in the Tottenham hot-seat for just four months admitted that some of the club's troubles were self-inflicted.

"Football is all about living on a knife-edge and as a manager that edge is much keener," said Burkinshaw, who took over from Terry Neill in the summer.

"I'm no quitter. I'll keep battling on. Some of my headaches are, I suppose, self-

inflicted because I refuse to turn away from attacking.

"I would hate to be in charge of a side that defended for 90 minutes. Perhaps that's been partly our downfall.

"But I'm not downhearted. If there was no hope I might as well pack it in right now.

"I certainly don't regret taking the job. Despite our problems I'm enjoying it. Maybe the bad times have come

first so I can enjoy the good times later."

Tottenham are second from bottom in the First Division, two points clear of West Ham but they hope to start a revival with a win over Stoke at White Hart Lane tomorrow.

And Burkinshaw gave his £200,000 winger Peter Taylor a vote of confidence.

"I've no plans to drop Peter," declared Burkinshaw.

No players' revolt says McFarland

By DAVID MOORE

DERBY skipper Roy McFarland said yesterday that there was no dressing room revolt behind the sacking of manager Dave Mackay.

The England centre half, who has shaken off a knee injury to take his place in today's game against fellow strugglers Sunderland, said in a statement:

"I want to make it clear there has been no

sinister dressing room influence on the boardroom decision.

"Obviously the players must take some of the responsibility for our League position. Dave Mackay has said that he was not given 100 per cent by everyone in some matches.

"Now, we have got to

start sorting things out right away. I don't think Derby will ever be relegation candidates, but it is important that we begin getting our results right."

"Everybody will be looking at Derby's performances because of what has just happened.

"This probably puts

even more responsibility than ever on the players —but we are all confident that we can handle it."

Caretaker manager Colin Murphy, the former reserve team coach will give Bruce Rioch and Kevin Hector fitness tests this morning on their injured ankles before naming his first line-up.

But the signs are that he has already decided to scrap one Mackay idea and move Colin Todd from midfield to central defender alongside McFarland.

Printed and Published by THE DAILY MIRROR NEWSPAPERS Ltd., (01-353 0246) at, and for Mirror Group Newspapers Ltd., Holborn Circus, London, E C1P 1DQ. Registered at the Post Office as a newspaper

---

Derby finished fourth in the 1975–76 campaign despite manager Dave Mackay's predictions towards the end of the previous season that, if they won that one, they would win this one, too. And when his team made a disappointing start to the 1976–77 season cracks began to appear in his reign. On Thursday, 25th November, with Derby having won just two of the opening 13 league games, Mackay asked the board for a vote of confidence, which he didn't get. He was duly sacked, a little more than three years after he had replaced Brian Clough. Rumours surfaced of a dressing-room revolt but Roy McFarland moved quickly to quash them. Later, Mackay said: "Dave Mackay sacked himself."

Rams' reserve team coach Colin Murphy took over following Mackay's dismissal, with Dario Gradi installed as his number two, although the pair would last less than a year. Derby finished 15th in the 1976–77 season, and the two men were sacked the following September. Not that they didn't leave their mark on the club. Their last home game in charge was the record 12-0 victory at the Baseball Ground over Irish side Finn Harps in the UEFA Cup on 15th September. Kevin Hector scored five times, with Charlie George and Leighton James bagging a hat-trick apiece, and Bruce Rioch was also on target. George, pictured scoring Derby's sixth in the first leg, and Hector scored two goals each in the second leg a fortnight later, which Derby won 4-1. By the time of the second leg Murphy and Gradi were no longer in Derby's employ. Two days after the first game, they strolled along Shaftesbury Crescent (right) and into the Baseball Ground to be told their services were no longer required.

The three musketeers

ARSENAL! WHO ARE THEY?

DEREK HALES makes his First Division debut tonight neither knowing, nor caring, who will be marking him.

Says Derby's £300,000 signing: "I'm looking forward to it — but I've no idea who Arsenal have in their defence.

"I think Pat Rice and Peter Simpson still play, but I couldn't tell you who their centre half is."

So while the football world is agog to see if he can carry on his phenomenal scoring ability at the Baseball Ground tonight Hales is treating it as "just another game."

Approach

His down-to-earth approach has protected him from the ballyhoo which has surrounded his arrival in the First Division at the comparatively late age of 24.

He adds: "It wouldn't bother me if I had been transferred for £10,000. If people say I'm not worth £300,000, £200,000 or £100,000, then so what?"

By DAVE HORRIDGE

The drama of recent events at Derby were revealed by Colin Murphy, the acting manager whose signing of Hales was his first transfer deal.

Said Murphy: "Only four years ago I played against Derek when I was at Gravesend and he was with Dartford. They beat us 2-1 and neither of us could have dreamt I would be managing him in the First Division in such a short space of time."

Murphy, a great advocate of coaching, admits: "There is no way anybody could coach the scoring instinct that Derek possesses.

"He will probably find it harder in the First Division, but he has the strength, ability, courage and confidence to get goals in any League."

For a big-money buy Hales has had a remarkable career. At sixteen he was an amateur with West Ham. Then he played for Faversham in the Kent League, and after an unsuccessful trial at Norwich, joined Dartford.

At nineteen he signed pro for Luton, and moved to Charlton for £6,000. Only when manager Andy Nelson arrived did he get regular first team football, and he admits: "I suddenly realised I was worth money.

"But I didn't push to get away. If nobody had come in with something like £300,000 I would have stayed at Charlton."

Incidentally, Arsenal's back four tonight reads: Rice, David O'Leary, Pat Howard and Sammy Nelson. Alan Hudson, their £200,000 signing from Stoke, is not playing because of a stomach strain.

Derby snapped up Derek Hales – whose goalscoring exploits at Charlton, where he had terrorized defences, earned him the nickname "Killer" – in 1976, and on his arrival in the East Midlands he posed between his new strike partners Charlie George (left) and Leighton James. Hales cost £300,000 but unfortunately he struggled in the top flight, scoring just four league goals in 23 appearances for the Rams. He was sold to West Ham after just one season.

Tommy Docherty arrives at the Baseball Ground on 19th September 1977, two days after taking over as manager of Derby. Inset, "The Doc" is pictured in his office at the stadium on 12th January 1978.

Tommy Docherty spent just 20 months at the helm, a period in which several of the club's established star names, including Colin Todd, Kevin Hector, David Nish and Ron Webster, left the Baseball Ground. Derby finished 12th in The Doc's first season, and one place above relegation in the second. Docherty was sacked at the end of that season and replaced by former Nottingham Forest player Colin Addison. Addison's first season saw the club relegated, finishing second from bottom in the First Division, and while they were sixth in the Second Division the following campaign, they began the 1981–82 season poorly. Addison was sacked midway through, with Derby eventually finishing 16th.

Addison on the hallowed Baseball Ground turf with the club mascot in December 1979.

Derby players accused

TAYLOR SLAMS 'CHEATS'

ANGRY: Derby manager Peter Taylor

By DAVID MOORE

PETER TAYLOR lashed out last night at the "cheats and spivs" who are endangering his job as Derby manager.

With Derby anchored in the Second Division relegation zone, Taylor said: "We've sunk so low, non-League Telford must now start favourites against us in next Saturday's fourth round FA Cup tie!

"But I am not blaming lack of finance, loss of form or anything else for the way we have betrayed our fans

"It is all down to the cheats who are placing the club's survival and my job at risk.

"We cannot afford a single new player on loan, so I have no alternative about picking some of them against Telford."

Stan Storton, boss of Alliance Premier League side Telford, said: "Mr. Taylor must be joking, although it's quite clear he is under pressure. A side like Derby should always beat us."

Taylor, with more than two years left of his contract added: "We would certainly be good enough if everybody here was honest enough. Certain players are spivving their way through games.

"I can't wait until the season ends, then I can kick them all out."

Taylor was backed by skipper Archie Gemmill—Derby's outstanding performer—and star signing John Robertson.

Robertson said: "It's heartbreaking. I believed I was joining a promotion team, instead of one staring Third Division soccer in the face."

Gemmill, 37, said: "Perhaps the management have made mistakes, too. Yet if you are an honest professional, you put matters behind you on the pitch and do the business for the fans who pay your wages."

DERBY

Rise and fall of a manager

PETER TAYLOR was a goalkeeper with Coventry, Middlesbrough and Port Vale, before going into management with non-League Burton.

● 1965—Brian Clough and Taylor in charge at Hartlepool.

● 1967—Clough and Taylor appointed by Derby.

● 1969—Second Division champions.

● 1972—First Division champions.

● 1973—European Cup semi-finalists, but trouble is brewing . . . October, Clough and Taylor resign . . . November, they join Brighton.

● 1974—The partnership splits up, and Clough goes to Leeds.

● 1976—Taylor rejoins Clough, now at Forest.

● 1978—League title and League Cup winners.

● 1979—European Cup and League Cup winners.

● 1980—European Cup and European Super Cup winners.

● 1982—Taylor quits Forest, claiming "mental exhaustion" . . . becomes Derby manager six months later.

McFARLAND: Nine games to avoid the drop

AXE TAYLOR

Now the pressure is on McFarland as he takes over

PETER TAYLOR quit trouble-torn Derby yesterday, leaving team manager Roy McFarland with nine games to save his job.

McFarland moves into the hot seat, with Derby languishing 20th in the Second Division, eight points adrift of the nearest safety spot. And he has little time to work an even bigger miracle than the one Taylor achieved to save Derby from relegation last season.

The threat was clear enough in a club statement which said: "Roy is in charge until the end of the season, at which time the board of directors will analyse the club's overall position and formulate future plans."

By DAVID MOORE

The statement was issued by Derby's major shareholder, Stuart Webb, who took over as chairman three hours before the departure of Taylor.

McFarland, 35, said he was "sick and upset" by Taylor's departure and admitted: "I wish Stuart had told me I would keep control during the two years remaining on my contract.

"But I couldn't expect that. In fact, I feel a certain sense of relief about not being asked to leave along with Peter. He brought me here and I must obviously share responsibility for our poor results."

McFarland, who cost Derby a £10,000 League fine plus £55,000 compensation after they poached him and coach Mick Jones—already dismissed—from Bradford City, added: "While there is still a mathematical chance of beating the drop, we must battle on."

Despite reaching the FA Cup quarter-finals, Derby have

IN: Greeted by ex-chairman Mike Watterson

OUT: Taylor leaves the Baseball Ground yesterday

won only one Second Division match this year.

Taylor, 55, whose contract was terminated by mutual consent, said: "Recent results have crucified me, together with adverse publicity, which was affecting my family.

"The length of many playing contracts proved a noose round my neck.

"I was snookered. There were six men in our line-up at Barnsley who I tried to get rid of on the very first day I arrived."

Derby spent more than £500,000 on transfers under Taylor, and finished up with an even worse team. In the end, he accepted "nominal" compensation for the 24 months remaining on his £22,000-a-year agreement.

DERBY SAVED

But the outlook's grim for Taylor

MIRROR SPORT last Tuesday

The early Eighties were not a good time for Derby who, with financial problems never a million miles away, regularly changed managers. John Newman lasted just 11 months before he was replaced by an old favourite, Peter Taylor. This time Taylor, who had quit as Brian Clough's assistant at Nottingham Forest six months earlier, was the main man rather than the trusted lieutenant but, restricted by finances and with players he did not feel were good enough or cared enough, his return would prove an ill-fated one. He left Derby by mutual consent in April 1984, leaving Roy McFarland, who had been brought in as his number two, nine games to save the club from relegation to the Third Division. It had been an awful season for the club, one of the worst in its history, with the threat of extinction looming large. A winding-up order from the High Court was lifted with the Maxwell family stepping in. On the field, however, problems continued to mount and, with McFarland unable to perform a miracle, the Rams once again dropped down to the third tier of English football.

Mirror Sport

Friday, March 2, 1984   No. 24,892
Telephone: (STD Code 01) — 353 0246

SINKING

Keep cool, fellows

MORGAN

From CHRIS LANDER in Paris

ENGLAND rugby fans were warned last night of a frightening backlash here following the crowd violence at the France-England soccer match.

More than 5,000 rugby supporters can expect a hostile anti-British attitude from the French public when they arrive for the Five Nations championship game tomorrow.

French Rugby Federation spokesman Jean Bertranne said: "People are utterly fed up with the antics of the so-called England sports fans. First they turned the place upside down when Tony Sibson fought for the European middleweight title.

"Now their soccer followers have damaged our stadium and have gone on the rampage through Paris."

Derek Morgan, chairman of the England rugby selectors, said: "Our followers had better be on their best behaviour. They should be careful not to give offence."

ENGLAND MATCH VERDICT—Page 31.

£1 million by noon or you're dead, Charlton

By JACK STEGGLES

CHARLTON will go out of business today...unless they find £1 million by lunchtime.

That bleak prospect faces the Sunley consortium, who took control yesterday after Mark Hulyer finally caved in to the pressure and quit as chairman.

The money is needed to meet stringent Football League requirements—and must be paid before Charlton Athletic (1984) will be allowed to do business.

Deposit

The new bosses have to find:
● Fully paid share capital of £350,000 to be subscribed in cash.
● A cash deposit of £50,000 from every director.
● Money owed to the League, preferential creditors plus Inland Revenue and Customs and Excise to be paid in full before admission.
● Seventy per cent to League club creditors and 60 per cent to unsecured creditors within two months.

Those requirements came as a devastating blow to the new consortium—headed by property developers Sunley—who were ready to move in following Tuesday's High Court winding up order.

They held an emergency meeting last night and solicitor Peter Crystal said: "The League presented us with a list of demands, such as the consent of the FA and PFA to the take-over. There was no problem on that.

"We agreed the terms with solicitors representing the League. Then an hour later, they rang back to say that League approval for a registration of Charlton Athletic (1984) would not be forthcoming unless a substantial sum—in excess of £1 million—was deposited with them tomorrow.

"This is clearly impractical, and our understanding is that it represents a change from what has previously been League policy in situations like this.

And Crystal added: "We question whether the League wish to succeed in this venture. Are they wanting us to be the first to go and, inevitably, accelerate the demise of other clubs?"

But League secretary Graham Kelly emphatically denied any change of policy. "We laid down our conditions to Charlton back in October and re-affirmed them this week. They are the same terms that applied in the cases of Wolves and Bristol City.

"Certain conditions have to be met. So far they have not, and until they are there can be no question of Charlton playing on."

Charlton are due to play at Blackburn tomorrow and Kelly added:

Resigned

"It's rubbish to suggest we want them to die. But this has to be sorted out one way or the other in the next few hours. And it will be."

Hulyer had resigned earlier in the day believing the new group would immediately step in and save the club with a £1½ million rescue act.

But the two-tier take-over, which had the blessing of the main creditor former chairman Mike Gliksten, is now in jeopardy.

HULYER: He quit as chairman.

GLIKSTEN: Approved of new consortium.

■ Hepworths ■

JACKET £24·95

YOU KNOW THE NAME..

SAVED

Maxwell to the rescue

By TONY STENSON

MILLIONAIRE Robert Maxwell, the Oxford chairman who failed to buy his way into Manchester United, is now ready to rescue Derby.

He agreed to put up the cash and revive the ailing fortunes of the famous Midlands club.

Derby, buckling under debts of £1.5 million, face a winding-up order in the High Court on March 12 for unpaid tax bills of £129,000. But Maxwell, anxious to elevate himself from small-time Oxford, will take up the challenge provided the deal is approved by all authorities.

He will immediately become chairman with Stuart Webb, who has been desperately trying to find financial backers, becoming paid managing director.

"I know many people have called him a robber baron but to us he's a shining white knight," said former chairman Webb.

Manager Peter Taylor, who has been given a vote of confidence, said: "Naturally I am absolutely delighted that the club looks like being saved. It is a tremendous relief, after living for so long with the threat of closure hanging over our heads.

"Now it is up to everybody in the club to respond and pull out all the stops to keep us in the Second Division."

Webb added: "We are delighted with Maxwell's intervention. It's 13th time lucky for us. He has had a dozen offers from First and Second Division clubs to help out, but he has gone where most needed.

"Mr. Maxwell believes Derby is worth it—it's certainly not a joy-ride for him."

Maxwell, who has interests locally in Rolls-Royce and publishing, said through a spokesman: "My offer is serious. I'm not seeking publicity. I'm making a real commitment."

Webb travelled to London yesterday to try to bring forward Derby's winding-up order. He said: "the sooner we put forward our package the sooner we can get clearance and begin the reconstruction of Derby."

Maxwell has also admitted that Oxford could close down within a year, and he spelt out his message of gloom in his chairman's report.

He had hoped for local council support to convert the Third Division club's ground into a multi-purpose leisure and living centre.

But he says: "If, after 30 years, the Oxford City Council continues to block and prevaricate, we will be closed down possibly by the end of this season and certainly not later than the end of next."

SAVIOUR: Maxwell

> " I had a great time at Derby and met some great characters – Roy McFarland, Gordon Guthrie – and without a shadow of doubt Arthur Cox was one of the most important influences on my career. He drummed it into me that, as a striker, the harder I worked, the luckier I would get. He emphasised how important it was never to stop working on or off the field. Arthur used to wait in the tunnel at half-time and tell opposing defenders, 'If you think you're knackered now, there's 45 minutes more of that to come, he's the fittest striker in the league.' I had a great time at Derby and scored quite a lot of goals. "
>
> Dean Saunders

Arthur Cox's Black-and-White Army
1984-1993

1984–85 Arthur Cox takes over as manager, with Roy McFarland as his number two; the club finish seventh but the following year claim third, to win promotion back to the Second Division. **1986–87** Cox makes it back-to-back promotions, with Bobby Davison on fire in front of goal in both seasons. John Gregory and Phil Gee are also goalscoring heroes as the Rams win the league; Robert Maxwell had helped rescue the club in 1984 and he took over as chairman, signing England stars Peter Shilton and Mark Wright, for a record fee. **1988–89** Derby break the £1 million barrier for the first time to snap up Wales striker Dean Saunders. He is an instant hit with the fans, scoring five goals in his first four games and bagging 14 in 30 games, as Derby finish fifth. The Rams are denied European football because of the ban on English clubs following the Heysel disaster. **1990–91** Chairman Maxwell ushers in a freeze on transfers and Cox's side suffer a 20-game winless run, a record for the club, which contributes largely to their relegation from the First Division; Saunders and Wright are sold to Liverpool for a combined £5 million. **1991–92** In November, Maxwell is found dead in the Atlantic Ocean after allegedly falling overboard; that month local businessman Lionel Pickering pays £1 million to buy the club. He spends big and the Rams reach the play-offs. **1992–93** Derby pay Notts County £2.65 million for Craig Short, a record transfer fee paid by a club outside the top flight; Derby return to Wembley for the first time since 1975 but lose the Anglo-Italian Cup final to Cremonese. **1993** Cox resigns in October, citing ill health.

Arthur Cox arrived at the Baseball Ground at the start of the 1984–85 campaign and immediately set about stopping the rot which had set in at the club and seen Derby drop into the Third Division. Cox is pictured here with assistant-manager Roy McFarland and director Stuart Webb in October 1985 and, by May 1986, he was still smiling, as his side had secured promotion back to the Second Division.

> *If people ask who was the best manager I worked for I say there were two: Arthur Cox and Jock Wallace. I got in so much trouble but Arthur would always mask it up. He was like a dad to me as well. As a person, a bloke, I had so much respect for him.*
>
> Ted McMinn

Cox built on the previous season's success and steered Derby straight through the Second Division to win back-to-back promotions. Here the players celebrate their return to the top tier of English football after beating Plymouth Argyle 4-2 on 9th May 1987. They are, back row, from left to right: Michael Forsyth, Mark Lillis, Bobby Davison and Rob Hindmarch. Front row, left to right: Phil Gee, Nigel Callaghan, Geraint Williams, John Gregory, Paul Blades and Eric Steele.

The team and management staff go down on their knees to acclaim benefactor Robert Maxwell, the then-*Mirror* owner, who had saved the club.

Manager Arthur Cox enjoys the acclaim inside a jubilant Baseball Ground.

Arthur Cox might have been the man in the Derby hot seat, and Brian Clough might by this time have been in charge of Nottingham Forest, but Cloughie still felt an attachment to his former club and was still always in the media. He couldn't resist a sly dig at his own directors in a *Mirror* column while praising Cox, McFarland and director Stuart Webb for their achievements as Derby stood on the brink of their return to the First Division in May 1987.

With Derby back in the big time and with Maxwell's money to spend, Arthur Cox set about buying a new spine for his team and made a huge statement when he snapped up England goalkeeper Peter Shilton. Shilts, signed from Southampton and with 91 caps to his name, larks about with Cox at the Raynesway training centre after putting pen to paper under Maxwell's watchful eye at the businessman's *Mirror* office.

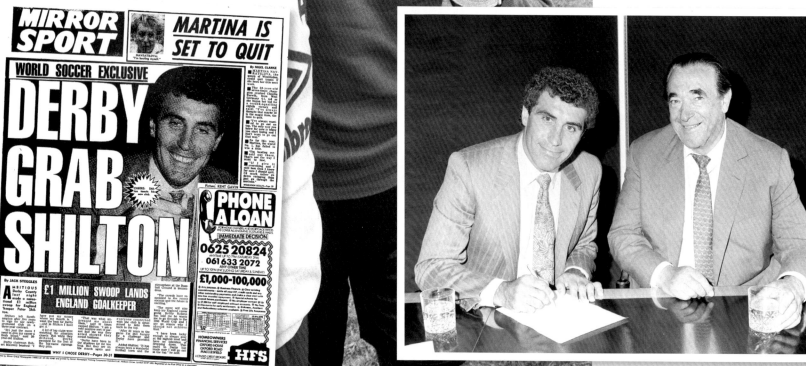

Ooh, Mark Wright ...

Cox (left), Robert Maxwell and managing director Stuart Webb (right) pose for pictures with Mark Wright in Maxwell's office at *Mirror* HQ.

Cox and Maxwell made it a double raid on Southampton that summer when they signed England centre-half Mark Wright for £760,000 just a couple of months after agreeing terms with Shilton. Wright eventually became Derby captain and was a hit with the fans, as much for the fact he liked to mix it with opponents as the elegant way he played the game. Powerful in the air, mobile and at ease with the ball at his feet, Wright was a fine all-round defender and was voted Derby's Player of the Season two years running, at the end of the 1988–89 and 1989–90 campaigns. He went on to enjoy a successful spell at Liverpool when he was sold for £2.1 million as part of the joint deal which took him and Dean Saunders to Anfield in 1991.

Back in the top flight and ahead of a First Division game with Chelsea at the Baseball Ground in November 1987, Derby's line-up, back row from left to right, is: Dave Penney, Ross McLaren, Andy Garner, Geraint Williams, Paul Blades, Brian McCord, Peter Shilton. Front row, left to right: Steve Cross, Michael Forsyth, Mark Wright, Robert Maxwell (owner), John Gregory, Nigel Callaghan, Phil Gee.

175

–LEGENDS–

Ted McMinn

Nicknamed the "Tin Man", McMinn was a throwback to the days of old-fashioned wingers and a real cult hero with Rams fans. He wore his distinct mullet hairstyle in homage to his own hero, Chris Waddle, and was a real character in the dressing room as well. His time at Derby was hampered by injuries and he was a regular on physio Gordon Guthrie's treatment table. A broken leg cost him a place in the Scotland squad at the 1990 World Cup in Italy. McMinn arguably came back from that injury a better player and won the 1991–92 Player of the Year award, as voted by Derby fans. After retiring, he suffered a mystery infection in his right foot, which led to him having his leg amputated below the knee. He raised £15,000 for charity – half went to Derbyshire Royal Infirmary's limbs unit and the other half to former Rangers chairman David Murray's Murray Foundation – by cycling from Ibrox to Pride Park following his two operations. A tribute game to McMinn took place between Derby and Rangers on 1st May 2006, and the Pride Park crowd that day was 33,475, a record for the stadium. An estimated 10,000 Rangers fans travelled to Derby for the game, and the two sets of supporters mingled freely in support of their former hero.

FOOTBALL
–STATS–

Ted McMinn

Name: Kevin Clifton "Ted" McMinn

Born: 28th September 1962 (Castle Douglas)

Playing career: Queen of the South, Rangers, Seville, Derby County, Birmingham, Burnley

Position: Winger

Derby appearances: 152 (1988–93)

Derby goals: 14

Sometimes people would say to me, 'How did you do that?' And I'd think, 'I haven't got a clue.' It was instinct and half the time it would come off, the other times I'd miss the ball and end up on my face.

Ted McMinn

177

Geraint "George" Williams helps Nigel Callaghan celebrate his goal in the 1-0 victory over West Ham at the Baseball Ground in February 1988, with then-Hammer Paul Ince in the background.

Mark Wright is put under pressure at White Hart Lane on 1ˢᵗ March 1988 during a 0-0 draw in the First Division with Tottenham (above), while Phil Gee attacks West Ham's defence on 27ᵗʰ February of that season (below). Nigel Callaghan, behind Gee in the photo, scored the only goal of the game. Derby finished the season 15ᵗʰ.

Gary Micklewhite looks on as John Gregory, who would go on to manage Derby between January 2002 and March 2003, lets fly against Southampton at the Baseball Ground on 23rd April 1988, a 2-0 win in which Gregory and Frank Stapleton scored.

DERBY COUNTY		VISITORS	
1	PETER SHILTON	1	JOHN BURRIDGE
2	RUSS MACLAREN	2	GERRY FORREST
3	MEL CASE	3	DEREK STATHAM
4	GORDON WILLIAMS	4	JIMMY CASE
5	MARK WRIGHT	5	KEVIN MOORE
6	ROB HINDMARCH	6	KEVIN BOND
7	GARY MICKLEWHITE	7	GRAHAM BAKER
8	FRANK STAPLETON	8	GLENN COCKERILL
9	PHIL GEE	9	COLIN CLARKE
10	JOHN GREGORY	10	ANDY TOWNSEND
11	NIGEL CALLAGHAN	11	ALAN SHEARER
12	LEWIS (MICK) PENNEY (DAVID)	12	D WALLACE R WALLACE
REFEREE	K S HACKETT		
LINESMEN			

ABOVE: The old Derby County chalkboard reveals the two line-ups for that game, with both sides able to call on some big names.

–LEGENDS–

Dean Saunders

Saunders became Derby's first seven-figure signing in October 1988 and made an immediate impact on the fans, scoring twice on his debut against Wimbledon and finding the net five times in his first four games. His goals that season would help Derby finish an impressive fifth in the First Division, and he followed up with 11 more the following campaign and another 17 the season after that. He teamed up superbly with strike partner Paul Goddard, but the pair didn't get to play together for as long as fans would have liked. Sadly, Saunders' goals in the 1990–91 season, at the end of which he won the Player of the Year award, weren't enough to keep Derby off bottom spot and, when they were relegated, he was sold to Liverpool for £2.9 million.

Saunders celebrates his goal in a 2-1 victory over Nottingham Forest at the Baseball Ground on 24th November 1990. Craig Ramage was the other goalscorer in a victory over the old enemy that would prove to be one of the few highlights during a poor campaign, which saw Derby finish bottom of the table and relegated to the Second Division.

LEFT: How the *Mirror* reported his arrival.

Saunders scores against Tottenham Hotspur in a 2-1 win in the 1989–90 season.

FOOTBALL
–STATS–

Dean Saunders

Name: Dean Nicholas Saunders

Born: 21st June 1964 (Swansea)

Playing career: Swansea, Cardiff (loan), Brighton, Oxford, Derby, Liverpool, Aston Villa, Galatasaray, Nottm Forest, Sheffield United, Benfica, Bradford City

Position: Forward

Managerial career: Wrexham, Doncaster

Derby appearances: 131 (1988–91)

Derby goals: 57

Wales appearances: 75

Wales goals: 22

Saunders with Arthur Cox after joining the club.

Paul "Jossie" Williams – nicknamed after Brazil legend Josimar – decides there's only one way to stop Paul Gascoigne during a game against Tottenham on 8th September 1990. Gazza bagged a hat-trick at White Hart Lane that day, as Derby were beaten 3-0.

185

SOCCER LOVER: Robert Maxwell salutes the fans during his successful time as chairman of Derby County

Lionel's millions

Robert Maxwell came into Derby as the club's saviour and was lauded for spending big money on big names early in his reign. By the time of his death, however, he was viewed as a pariah by Rams fans. He had shelled out on England internationals Peter Shilton and Mark Wright, and later striker Dean Saunders, but then, during 1990, he ushered in a transfer freeze which contributed greatly to Derby's relegation from the First Division, before announcing he was looking for a buyer for the club.

Maxwell's stock hit an all-time low with Rams fans when he sold Saunders and Wright to Liverpool for a combined £5 million and pocketed the cash in the summer of 1991, although the money did help push through the deal which saw a local consortium take charge of the club. Maxwell died the following November, his body found floating in the Atlantic, and the minute's silence which was held at the Baseball Ground following his death was met with contempt from many home fans, who booed, jeered and chanted against the late Czech businessman. Of course, there was devastation at the *Mirror*, which Maxwell had owned, and the newspaper ran several pages reflecting on his life and times, including a tribute from Peter Shilton, Maxwell's first big signing for Derby.

At the same time as Maxwell's death in 1991, local businessman Lionel Pickering introduced massive additional funding to the club which saw the Baseball Ground – indeed, the whole county – gripped by excitement. In the early part of 1992 it seemed big-money signings were being made on an almost weekly basis, with Marco Gabbiadini snapped up for £1 million from Crystal Palace, Leicester City's Paul Kitson valued at £1.3 million in a players-plus-cash deal which saw Ian Ormondroyd and Phil Gee move the other way, Tommy Johnson arriving for another £1.3 million from Notts County and Paul Simpson, with his cultured left foot, joining from Oxford for £500,000.

Derby made the play-offs that season but, despite their big spending, were beaten in the semi-finals by a Blackburn Rovers side who were themselves splashing then-owner Jack Walker's cash. Derby continued to spend, with Mark Pembridge costing £1.25 million from Luton Town in the 1992–93 campaign, Darren Wassall bought from Nottingham Forest for £600,000, and £2.65 million – a record fee for a club outside the top division – lavished on Craig Short, the big centre-half from Notts County. Martin Kuhl's £800,000 price tag seemed paltry by comparison, but at the time manager Arthur Cox saw him as the final piece in his jigsaw.

Paul Simpson (left), Paul Kitson (8) and Marco Gabbiadini (right) congratulate Tommy Johnson after his goal against Blackburn in the play-off semi-final first leg at Ewood Park on 10th May 1992. Goals from Gabbiadini and Johnson put Derby two up inside a quarter of an hour, but Blackburn took a 4-2 lead into the second leg, which was played three days later. Derby won that game 2-1, with goals from Andy Comyn and Ted McMinn, but Kevin Moran's strike was enough to take Rovers into the final on aggregate.

LEFT: Jason Kavanagh, Marco Gabbiadini and Ted McMinn are all on hand as Paul Williams gets to grips with Blackburn bad boy David Speedie in the second leg at the Baseball Ground.

Darren Wassall slides in to tackle Newcastle's David Kelly, with Paul Kitson looking on during the first home game of the 1992–93 campaign, on 22nd August (right). Meanwhile, Paul Williams holds off Lee Clark (above), and Simon Coleman and Jason Kavanagh can't prevent Clark getting off a shot in the Geordies' 2-1 win (below). Mark Pembridge was the Rams' goalscorer that day.

189

Rams back at Wembley

The Rams returned to European action for the first time since 1976 when they took part in the 1992–93 Anglo-Italian Cup and, even though the tournament failed to attract huge crowds to the Baseball Ground, around 36,000 Derby fans made the trip to Wembley on 27th March 1993, to see their team take on US Cremonese in the final. Derby had beaten Notts County and Barnsley in the preliminary rounds before reaching the knockout stages from the same Group B as Cremonese. They had also played against two more Italian sides, Cosenza Calcio 1914 and Reggina Calcio, in that group stage. Derby drew 5-5 on aggregate with Brentford in the semi-finals, but secured their place at Wembley thanks to the away-goal rule after a 4-3 victory at Griffin Park. Unfortunately, there was to be no joy at Wembley, with Cremonese winning 3-1, the same scoreline by which they had beaten Derby in the group stage.

Mark Patterson wheels away in delight after seeing Marco Gabbiadini score for Derby.

ABOVE: Tommy Johnson lies grounded and Shane Nicholson looks on as Mark Pembridge does battle in midfield.

RIGHT: Derby fans crammed into Wembley for their first visit since 1975.

LEFT: Left to right, Richard Goulooze, Mark Pembridge and Michael Forsyth are gutted as they pay tribute to the Derby fans at the end of the game.

That Derby Pride
1994-2012

" I can't remember much about the goal but it was a great feeling. I just kept running and the celebrations were terrific. "

Stephen Pearson

1994 With Roy McFarland having taken charge following Cox's departure through ill health, the club finish sixth to qualify for the play-offs. But there's heartbreak at Wembley when local rivals Leicester beat Derby. **1995** Jim Smith is appointed manager and brings in Igor Štimac for £1.57 million, the club's second-highest fee, from Hajduk Split in the player's native Croatia. The Rams lose Štimac's first game 5-1 at Tranmere but then embark on a run which, 20 games later, take them to the top of English football's second tier, now called the First Division. Sunderland eventually pip Derby to the title but the Rams finish second to join them in promotion. It was also a significant season because the club had announced they would be leaving the Baseball Ground and moving to a new stadium at Pride Park at the end of the following campaign. **1996–97** Paul McGrath and Paulo Wanchope join the club, the latter scoring a great goal on his debut against Manchester United. Derby County bid an emotional and fond farewell to the Baseball Ground, with the final game there ending in a 3-1 defeat at the hands of Arsenal. Ashley Ward scores Derby's last goal on the hallowed turf. **1997–98** Ward then bags the first goal for Derby at Pride Park but, with Derby leading Wimbledon 2-1, the floodlights fail and the game is abandoned. Instead it's Stefano Eranio, the AC Milan legend who had signed for Derby in the summer, whose name enters the record books as the first scorer on the ground. The club finish eighth in the Premier League.

Derby might have enjoyed play-off final joy in 2006, but 12 years earlier there was despair for Tommy Johnson and everyone associated with the club when they lost 2-1 to local rivals Leicester City at the old Wembley.

1999 Argentinian Esteban Fuertes signs but, after a training break, is refused re-entry to the UK after irregularities were found with his passport. **2001** Former player Colin Todd replaces Jim Smith but doesn't last long and is replaced by another ex-Ram, John Gregory. He can't stave off relegation. Fabrizio Ravanelli was one of the big-name stars who stayed after the drop but his wages would play a large part in almost crippling the club financially. **2003–04** The club go into receivership as a new three-man consortium comes in, but the financial woes continue. **2004–05** Division One is renamed the Championship. **2005** Rod Stewart plays the first concert at Pride Park. **2006–07** Stephen Pearson scores the Wembley winner against West Bromwich Albion in the play-off final to take Derby back into the Premier League. **2007–08** Paul Jewell replaces Billy Davies as manager in November but the club embark on a 21-game run without a victory, which sees them relegated with a record low Premier League tally of just 11 points. **2008–09** Jewell quits as manager at the end of December and Nigel Clough takes over in January, 42 years after his dad occupied the Derby hot seat. **2011** Mason Bennett becomes the youngest debutant for Derby, aged 15 years and 99 days, in October 2011.

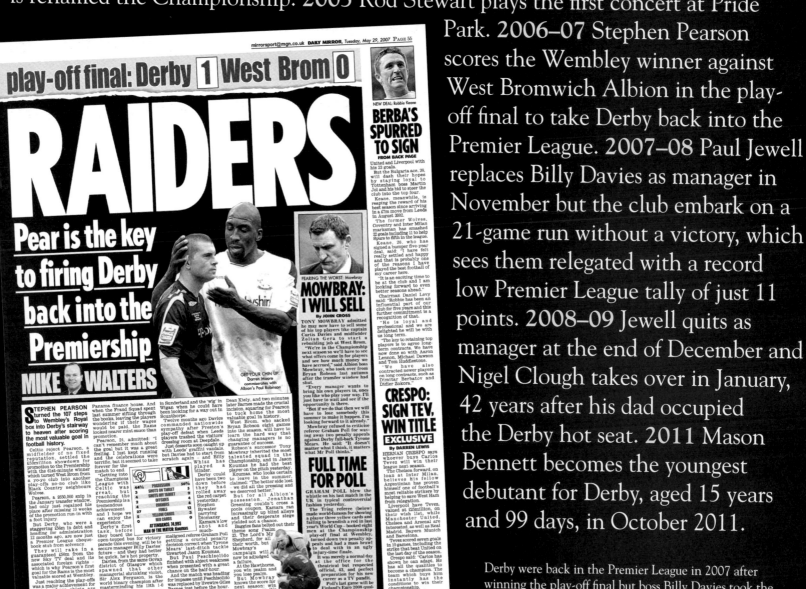

Derby were back in the Premier League in 2007 after winning the play-off final but boss Billy Davies took the opportunity to gripe at the board. He only lasted until the following November.

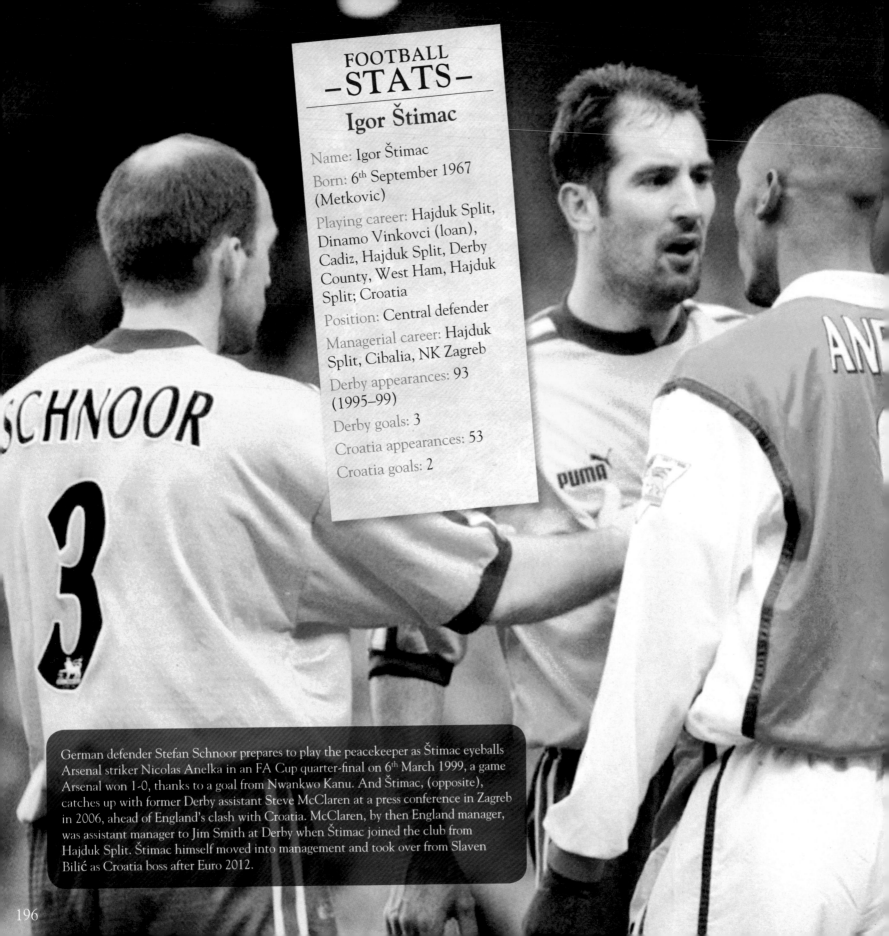

FOOTBALL
–STATS–

Igor Štimac

Name: Igor Štimac

Born: 6th September 1967 (Metkovic)

Playing career: Hajduk Split, Dinamo Vinkovci (loan), Cadiz, Hajduk Split, Derby County, West Ham, Hajduk Split; Croatia

Position: Central defender

Managerial career: Hajduk Split, Cibalia, NK Zagreb

Derby appearances: 93 (1995–99)

Derby goals: 3

Croatia appearances: 53

Croatia goals: 2

German defender Stefan Schnoor prepares to play the peacekeeper as Štimac eyeballs Arsenal striker Nicolas Anelka in an FA Cup quarter-final on 6th March 1999, a game Arsenal won 1-0, thanks to a goal from Nwankwo Kanu. And Štimac, (opposite), catches up with former Derby assistant Steve McClaren at a press conference in Zagreb in 2006, ahead of England's clash with Croatia. McClaren, by then England manager, was assistant manager to Jim Smith at Derby when Štimac joined the club from Hajduk Split. Štimac himself moved into management and took over from Slaven Bilić as Croatia boss after Euro 2012.

-LEGENDS-

Igor Štimac

Ask the Derby fans who were regular visitors to the Baseball Ground in the mid- to late Nineties to name their favourite Rams player and many will tell you, without a moment's hesitation, it was Igor Štimac. A wonderful talent, a real leader and hugely charismatic, Štimac topped a BBC poll of Derby fans in 2004 when they were asked to name their all-time cult hero. Štimac, who cost £1.57 million from his hometown club, Hajduk Split, scored on his Rams debut at Tranmere on 4th November 1995, although the game didn't end well for Derby, who were well beaten 5-1. However, they would then embark on a 20-match unbeaten run, which took the club to the top of the First Division. Derby were just pipped to the title by Sunderland, but second place was enough to secure promotion back to the top flight.

On Štimac's recommendation, manager Jim Smith moved for another Croatia international, Aljoša Asanović. It is incredible that the midfielder only played 35 games for Derby, such was the impact he had on the club. He was gifted with the most wonderful left foot and his ability to find team-mates with 40- and 50-yard passes was second to none.

Welcome to Pride Park

Derby legend Roy McFarland is pictured in the Pride Park stands in December 2008.

During the 1995–96 season, the club confirmed they would be leaving the Baseball Ground after 102 years. The famous old stadium had been the setting for some of the most memorable matches in Derby County's history, and will always be recalled with fondness by those who filed through its turnstiles. Its almost vertical stands were so close to the pitch that those who played there often said it felt like the crowd was on top of them. Time moves on, though, and the decision to build a new stadium became inevitable. The last league game was played at the Baseball Ground on 11th May 1997, a 3-1 defeat by Arsenal in the Premier League, in which striker Ashley Ward scored the last Derby goal. Ian Wright's second, scored after 90 minutes, was the final goal at the stadium.

So Derby moved into their new Pride Park home – officially opened by Queen Elizabeth II on 18th July 1997 – that summer. Italian giants Sampdoria provided the opposition for the first game at the new stadium, a pre-season friendly that ended in a 1-0 defeat on 4th August, before the Rams held their first competitive fixture at the ground against Wimbledon on Wednesday, 13th August. Ward thought he had written his name into the history books again when he scored Derby's first goal at the new stadium but, after 56 minutes and with the score 2-1 to the Rams, a power failure meant the floodlights went out and the game had to be abandoned. Stefano Eranio's goal in a 1-0 win over Barnsley the following Saturday was therefore recorded as the first competitive goal at the new stadium. In August 2010, the club unveiled a statue of Brian Clough and Peter Taylor outside Pride Park as a permanent reminder of the glory days of the late Sixties and early Seventies.

The foreign invasion

Gangly Costa Rican striker Paulo Wanchope was another Jim Smith signing who was an instant hit with Derby fans. He marked his Premier League debut with a goal against Manchester United in a 3-2 victory which would be voted the best in Derby's history by fans in 2009. His goal was Derby's second, with Ashley Ward and Dean Sturridge also on target. Dutchman Robin van der Laan arrived at the Baseball Ground before Wanchope, in the summer of 1995, and Smith made him captain. It was his goal against Crystal Palace, the crucial strike in a 2-1 win at the Baseball Ground at the end of the 1995–96 campaign, which secured his place in the Rams' record books as it earned them promotion to the Premier League. Other notable players from overseas included Stefano Eranio, the wonderfully talented former AC Milan and Italy midfielder-cum-winger, and Francesco Baiano, the diminutive striker who was also capped by Italy and had made his name with Foggia and Fiorentina in his homeland before joining the Rams. Georgian midfield ace Georgi Kinkladze and Croatia-born Belgium striker Branko Strupar were also firm favourites with the fans.

Wanchope celebrates a goal against Manchester City in the League Cup in 1998.

Despite the fact Derby fans were able to marvel at their talents, there was a downside to the club bringing in foreign stars on big salaries, particularly in the case of Fabrizio Ravanelli. The Italian's wages, believed to be in the region of £50,000 a week, almost brought the club to its knees, although Ravanelli, it seemed, was merely the straw that broke the camel's back. After all, the financial difficulties had been growing for some time. There were serious problems in the Eighties before the Maxwell family stepped in, and again in 1994 when Lionel Pickering's funds began to dry up. On the field, the early Noughties were not a particularly good period, either, with the club relegated back to the Championship at the end of the 2001–02 season.

Back in the big time …

Derby spent the next five seasons in the Championship and struggled in three of them, although they did reach the play-offs in 2004–05, where they lost to Preston in the semi-finals. In the 2006–07 campaign, however, they finished third and beat Southampton in the play-off semi-finals to set up a clash with West Bromwich Albion at Wembley in the showpiece final. Stephen Pearson scored the only goal of the game to give Derby victory over West Brom at Wembley. Billy Davies was the manager who took them up, but his relationship with the board hit rock bottom the following November and the club turned to Paul Jewell. It was a terrible season for Derby, who were relegated the following May with a record low for the Premier League of 11 points. The only positives were the sell-out crowds at Pride Park, which won the club major respect across the country.

Pearson slides in the winner (below), while midfielder Seth Johnson challenges Robert Koren (left). Captain Matt Oakley and manager Billy Davies are all smiles as they get their hands on the trophy (right and below right). The victory meant the focus was back on Robbie Savage and his Derby pals (far right) the following season as they returned to the big time.

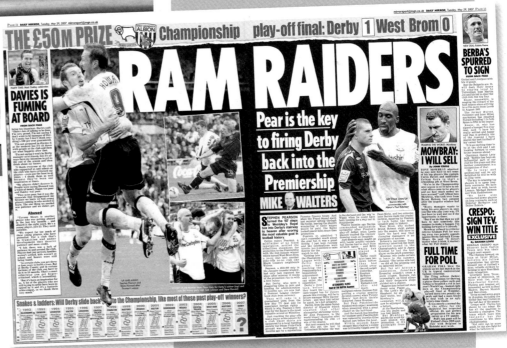

Robbie Savage joined the club in 2008 and went on to captain the Rams before retiring and embarking on a successful media career. In 2011, shortly after he had hung up his boots, Savage took part in the BBC programme *Strictly Come Dancing*. He and his partner, Ola Jordan, put on a show for fans at the Madejski Stadium ahead of Reading's game against Derby that November.

The Clough years: part II

In January 2008, after Paul Jewell parted ways with the club, Derby rolled back the years by employing a young manager whose family name was synonymous with the Rams. Nigel Clough had spent much of his childhood running around the corridors at the Baseball Ground while his dad, Brian, was manager and, 35 years on, after a fine playing career with Nottingham Forest, Liverpool and England, and an 11-year spell as manager of Burton Albion, he was part of the fabric of Derby County once again. Our inset pictures show Nigel, then 14, with his dad and Peter Taylor, who were in charge down the road from Derby at Forest at that point, and with dad and sister, Elizabeth, when Brian was in charge of Derby. Nigel was three at the time and would go on to witness first hand some incredible times at the club. Little did he know then that one day he would be given the chance to follow in his father's illustrious footsteps as manager of one of England's best-loved clubs.

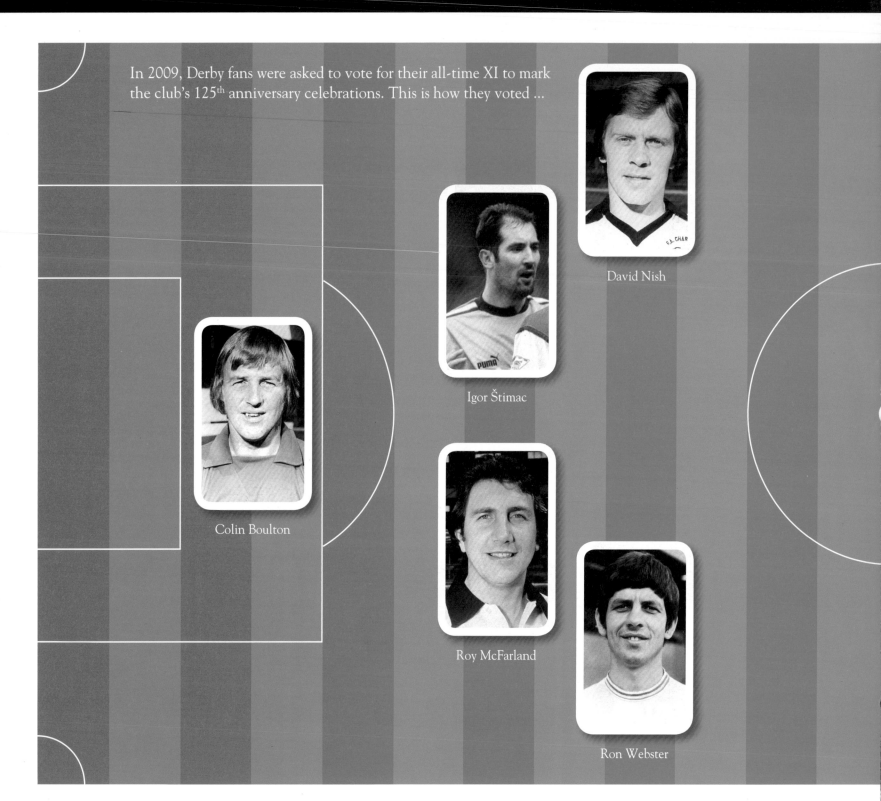

In 2009, Derby fans were asked to vote for their all-time XI to mark the club's 125th anniversary celebrations. This is how they voted ...

David Nish

Igor Štimac

Colin Boulton

Roy McFarland

Ron Webster

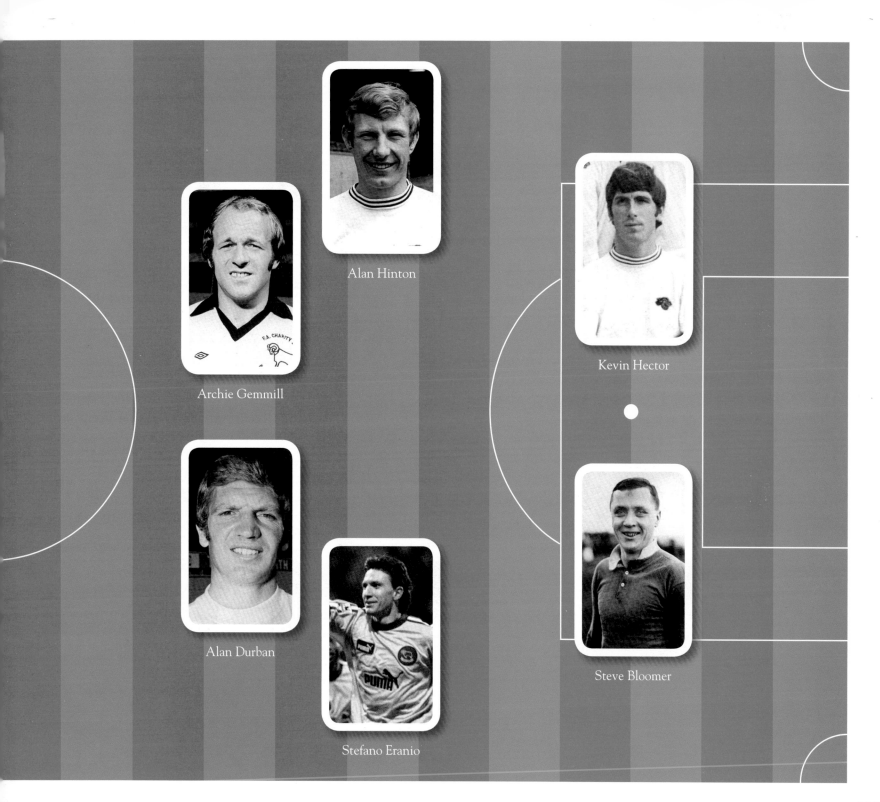

Alan Hinton

Archie Gemmill

Kevin Hector

Alan Durban

Stefano Eranio

Steve Bloomer

For Jane, Colin and Anne. Family, friends. Thank you for your support.

The author would also like to thank:
Richard Havers for the opportunity, and for his guidance, knowledge and suggestions; David Scripps, Vito Inglese and the team at Mirrorpix for their invaluable assistance; all at Haynes Publishing; and the staff at Derby Local Studies Library.

Special thanks again to Roy McFarland.
Sources: *Derby County: The Complete Record*, Gerald Mortimer; *The Little Book of Derby County*, Peter Seddon; *The Legends of Derby County*, Ian Hall; and *Destroying Angel, Steve Bloomer, England's First Football Hero*, Peter Seddon (all Breedon Books); *Bloomer and Before*, Edward Giles (The Hallamshire Press). *Nobody Ever Says Thank You*, Jonathan Wilson (Orion Books).
Newspapers: *Daily Mirror, Sunday Pictorial*. Website: www.dcfc.co.uk.

Lastly, thanks to Nigel Clarke, Peter Ingall, Frank McGhee, Dave Horridge, John Thompson, Monte Fresco, Dick Williams, Kent Gavin, Peter Lea, Roger Allen and all those *Mirror* men and women who have written about and photographed the East Midlands' finest club.